AA Explore

SOUTHERN ENGLAND

Tower Bridge by night

SOUTHERN ENGLAND

AA Publishing

Text and illustrations taken from the series *Explore Britain's...*, first published by the Automobile Association and the Daily Telegraph in 1993 and 1995:

Explore Britain's Castles by Elizabeth Cruwys and Beau Riffenburg
Explore Britain's Coastline by Richard Cavendish
Explore Britain's Country Gardens by Michael Wright
Explore Britain's Historic Houses by Penny Hicks
Explore Britain's National Parks by Roland Smith
Explore Britain's Steam Railways by Anthony Lambert
Explore Britain's Villages by Susan Gordon

Published by AA Publishing, a trading name of Automobile Association Developments Limited, whose registered office is Norfolk House, Priestley Road, Basingstoke, Hampshire RG24 9NY. Registered Number 1878835.

© The Automobile Association 1996

Maps © Advanced Illustration, Congleton 1996

A catalogue record for this book is available from the British Library.

ISBN 0 7495 1300 4

Colour origination by L.C. Repro & Sons Ltd, Aldermaston, England
Printed and bound in Italy by Tipolitografia G. Canale & C.S.p.A. – Turin

The contents of this book are believed correct at the time of printing. Nevertheless, the Publishers cannot accept responsibility for errors or omissions, or for changes in details given.

Acknowledgements:

AA PHOTO LIBRARY F/Cover A. Baker, B/Cover: a D. Forss, b P. Brown, c D. Forss, d W. Voysey, e, f D. Forss; 1 T. Wyles; 3, 7, P. Baker; 8, 9a, 9b D. Forss; 10 M. Birkitt; 11 D. Forss; 12, 13 S. & O. Mathews; 15 M. Birkitt; 16 M. Adleman; 17 S. & O. Mathews; 18, 19 M. Birkitt; 20, 21 M. Trelawny; 22 R. Surman; 23 M. Birkitt; 24, 25 S. & O. Mathews; 26 R. Mort; 27 M. Trelawny; 28 R. Mort; 29 R. Strange; 30 P. Baker; 31 W. Voysey; 32 M. Trelawny; 33 R. Mort; 34, 35, 36, 37 W. Voysey; 38, 39 D. Forss; 40/1 W. Voysey; 42, 43, D. Forss; 44, 45a, b, W. Voysey; 46/7, 47 R. Fletcher; 49, 50 S. & O. Mathews; 51, 52, 53, 54 W. Voysey; 55 D. Forss; 56 W. Voysey; 57 P. Eden; 58, 59 P. Baker; 60 M. Birkitt; 61 M. Adleman; 62, 63a, 63b, 64, 65 M. Birkitt; 66/7 W. Voysey; 67 A. Lawson; 68/9 V. Greaves; 69 N. Ray; 70 V. Greaves; 71 F. Stephenson; 72, 73a, 73b, 74, 75 D. Forss; 76/7, 77 D. Croucher; 78, 79 S. & O. Mathews; 80, 81a, 81b W. Voysey; 82 D. Forss; 83 D. Noble; 84, 85 S. & O. Mathews; 86, 87a, 87b D. Forss; 88 S. & O. Mathews; 89 D. Forss; 90 M. Trelawny; 91, 92/3, 93, 94 94/5, D. Forss; 96/7 P. Brown; 96, 98, 99, 100/1, 102, 103 D. Forss; 104 S. & O. Mathews; 105 W. Voysey; 106 D. Corrance; 107 P. Baker; 108 D. Noble; 109, 110, 111a, b, 112, 113 D. Forss; 114 S. & O. Mathews; 115 D. Forss; 116 P. Baker; 117 D. Forss; 118 S. & O. Mathews; 119 D. Noble; 120, 121, 122, 123 D. Forss; 124/5, 125, 126 D. Noble; 127 S. & O. Mathews

CONTENTS

&

SOUTHERN ENGLAND

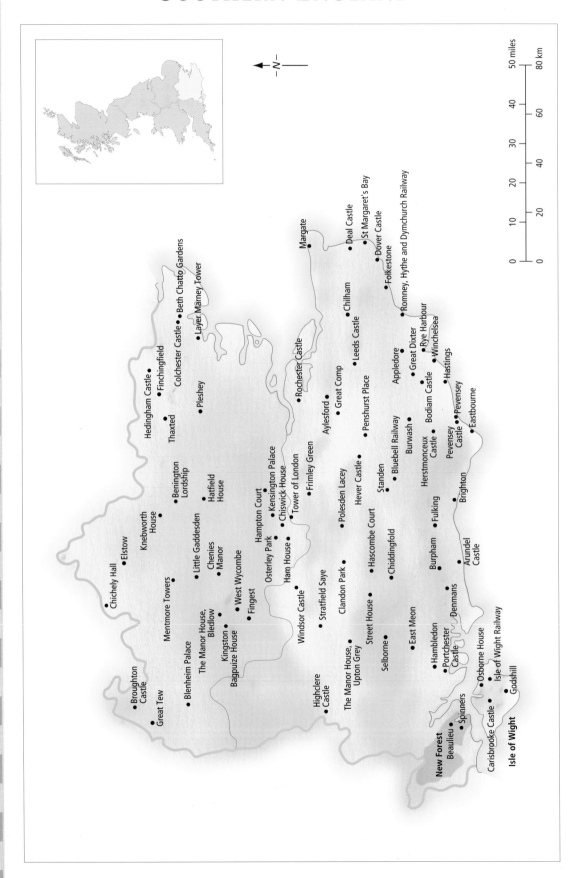

50 miles
80 km

0   10   20   30   40   50 miles
0   20   40   60   80 km

Margate
Deal Castle
St Margaret's Bay
Dover Castle
Folkestone
Romney, Hythe and Dymchurch Railway
Chilham
Leeds Castle
Rochester Castle
Great Comp
Aylesford
Penshurst Place
Great Dixter
Rye Harbour
Winchelsea
Hastings
Appledore
Burwash
Bodiam Castle
Pevensey
Pevensey Castle
Eastbourne
Bluebell Railway
Herstmonceux Castle
Standen
Hever Castle
Polesden Lacey
Brighton
Hascombe Court
Chiddingfold
Arundel Castle
Burpham
Fulking
Denmans
Colchester Castle   Beth Chatto Gardens
Layer Marney Tower
Hedingham Castle
Finchingfield
Thaxted
Pleshey
Benington Lordship
Hatfield House
Kensington Palace
Hampton Court
Chiswick House
Tower of London
Frimley Green
Knebworth House
Little Gaddesden
Chenies Manor
West Wycombe
Fingest
Osterley Park
Ham House
Windsor Castle
Stratfield Saye
Clandon Park
Street House
East Meon
Selborne
Hambledon
Portchester Castle
Osborne House
Isle of Wight Railway
Godshill
Carisbrooke Castle
Isle of Wight
Spinners
Beaulieu
New Forest
Highclere Castle
The Manor House, Upton Grey
Bagpuize House
Kingston
The Manor House, Bledlow
Mentmore Towers
Blenheim Palace
Broughton Castle
Great Tew
Chichely Hall
Elstow

– N –

ℐNTRODUCTION

*At little, huddled, neighbourly Rye, even a white December
sea-fog is a cosy and convenient thing.*

Henry James, 'Letter to W E Norris', 1900

The southern region of England just simply oozes gentility, evoking scenes of walks along the South Downs, stretching through Surrey and Sussex to the south coast, and lazy picnics amongst some of the most pleasing landscapes in the country. Even the term "The Home Counties' has a comforting feel to it – a feel that says much about this most English of regions.

Its many charming and historic villages may now be home to the armies of commuters working in the great sprawl that is London, itself swallowing parts of Essex and Kent in its continual growth, but nothing can detract from their inherent character. Whether in town or country, this region has it all, from the grandeur of the royal palaces of Hampton Court and Kensington Palace, to the often overlooked charms of old Essex and the diversities of the south- and east-coast resorts – elegant Arundel and Eastbourne, vibrant Brighton and Margate. Kent, called the garden of England, whose magnificent castles for centuries stood guard over its famous cliffs, now stands guard over the Channel Tunnel, gateway to Continental Europe,

The region is home to the ancient and historic New Forest, a National Park in all but name, with its famous ponies and other wildlife, perfect for losing yourself in peaceful surroundings, but never too far from the modern world. This is a truly wonderful region with something for everyone.

*My admiration of the New Forest is great:
it is true old wild English Nature,
and then the fresh heath-sweetened air is so delicious.
The Forest is grand.*

Alfred Lord Tennyson's diary of 1855,

from 'Alfred Lord Tennyson, a Memoir by his Son', 1897

THE MANOR HOUSE, BLEDLOW
Buckinghamshire

2½ MILES (4 KM) SOUTH-WEST OF PRINCES RISBOROUGH

The stately Manor House, with borders of roses and lavender

Nestling deep in the Buckinghamshire countryside below the Chiltern escarpment is the Manor House. A serene, brick house of the early 18th century, it stands in gardens of exceptional beauty created by the owners, Lord and Lady Carrington, with the help of the landscape architect, Robert Adams, in a style which is essentially English.

This is a garden of tremendous variety and elegance with a mixture of formal and informal enclosures. Along the width of the house, herbaceous borders planted with roses and lavender stretch out as if to emphasise the formal structure of the building, and, beyond the immaculate lawns, a line of rectangular lily ponds shows the reds, pinks and whites of many varieties of waterlily. Tall yew and beech hedges give a marvellous sense of enclosure for the yellow and white roses which contrast sharply with the blues and purples of lavender and heliotropium, while a sundial edged with box provides a central focus.

But the formal borders, filled not only with herbaceous flowers and shrubs but also with fragrant old roses, must be set against some equally enchanting informal areas. Here, you can sit and admire *Nicotiana sylvestris* towering over the bright colours of antirrhinums and fuchsias, and the stunning combination of tufts of silver santolina interplanted with purple heliotropium. Inside a walled kitchen garden, bright blue salvias, penstemons and peonies mingle with statuesque runner beans and other vegetables, and York stone paths lead to an enchanting, rose-covered gazebo.

A sculpture garden has recently been designed on a sloping site with wide open views: underneath mature trees, large modern figures playfully roll on the lawns, their white bodies contrasting with the spiky buddleia behind.

Although the gardens of the Manor House are only open on a very few days in the year, the tranquil Lyde Garden is worth going to at any time. Paths, bridges and walkways lead through this stunning water garden where there are many unusual species of plants.

Open by written appointment from May to September, and on selected afternoons. Lyde Garden is open every day.

Left, a tumbling stone figure from the sculpture garden

Below, a bench is discreetly placed to enjoy the borders

CHICHELEY HALL
Buckinghamshire

CHICHELEY, 2½ MILES (4 KM) NORTH-EAST OF NEWPORT PAGNELL

*I*t would be hard to find bricks put to better use than in the construction of Chicheley Hall – nearly a million were used in the house, its wings and its garden walls – and the pale colour of the pillars, doors and windows contrast to splendid effect. There is yet more contrast inside, as the warmth of the brickwork gives way to the cool, classical entrance hall, then the rich oak panelling of the drawing room, the library and Lord Beatty's study. The Jacobean Room, different again, contains 16th-century fragments from the previous house at Chicheley.

Built for the Chester family between 1719–23, the house had a chequered history, including use by the military and as a school. In 1952 it was bought by the 2nd Earl Beatty who turned it back into a beautiful home. His father, the 1st Earl, was one of the most outstanding and courageous naval commanders of this century. Awarded the DSO at the age of 25, he rose rapidly to become Admiral at the age of 45, and later First Sea Lord. He is, perhaps, best remembered as commander at the decisive Battle of Jutland in 1916. Lord Beatty's study contains his collections, including naval paintings, photographs and copies of his many decorations (the originals are in the Greenwich Naval Museum, London).

Open during April, May and August on Sunday and Bank Holiday afternoons. Tel: 01234 391252.

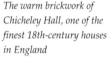
The warm brickwork of Chicheley Hall, one of the finest 18th-century houses in England

The Manor is offset by its magnificent garden

CHENIES MANOR
Buckinghamshire

4 MILES (6.5 KM) EAST OF AMERSHAM

A secret chamber, tunnels leading out into the woods, stories of royal visits – and even a royal ghost – all add to the fascination of this lovely 15th-century manor house. Queen Elizabeth I certainly did sleep here, on a number of occasions, and her father, Henry VIII, brought two of his wives here. They say that his ghostly footsteps can still sometimes be heard, painfully dragging his ulcerated legs along in an attempt to catch his queen, Catherine Howard, in the act of adultery with one of his attendants.

Chenies, built of mellow red brick with stepped gables and some of England's best examples of Tudor chimneys, was the work of the same team of men who enlarged Hampton Court for Henry VIII. The rooms within vary considerably: the oak-floored Queen Elizabeth's Room, with its 16th-century tapestries and furniture; the armoury, a primitive Long Gallery where troops were billeted during the Civil War; the delightful Blue Bedroom with its Chippendale four-poster and other 18th-century furniture; the dining room, modernised in the early 19th century and furnished in contemporary style. The stone parlour, now with 17th-century furniture, is thought to have been the original hall of the 15th-century house.

Open from April to October on selected afternoons. Tel: 01494 762888.

The previous building at Chenies once belonged to Edward I, who used it as a hunting box. Records of one visit in 1296 claim that he brought a camel with him! They also relate that 130 eggs were boiled and distributed to the villagers on Easter Day – possibly the first record of Easter eggs in Britain.

FINGEST
Buckinghamshire

6 MILES (9.5KM) SOUTH-WEST OF HIGH WYCOMBE

Tucked away in a deep, green valley in the Chilterns, Fingest has a particularly interesting Norman church. The flint and brick houses, cottages and farm buildings of the village – and, indeed, the main body of the church – are dwarfed by its large tower. It is early Norman, nearly 30 feet (9m) square, with walls over 3 feet (1m) thick, and most unusually has a twin-gabled roof above elaborately carved openings in the belfry. The present nave is not much narrower than the tower and is joined to it by a 12th-century arch. So large is the tower that it may originally have been the nave. The present chancel has no arch to it, being divided from the nave by a wooden screen in the 19th century, after restoration work was carried out. North of the churchyard are the remains of a palace of the Bishops of Lincoln, Buckinghamshire being at one time part of that bishopric. One of these bishops, Henry Burghersh, Bishop from 1320 to 1340, evidently was no friend of the needy and for his sins is doomed to wander the woods near by, a ghostly apparition dressed as a forester. South of the church is the 300-year-old chequered brick inn, a well-known hostelry.

The village in its setting deep among the beechwoods of the Chilterns

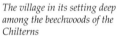

The stunning double colonnade

WEST WYCOMBE HOUSE
Buckinghamshire

3 MILES (5 KM) WEST OF HIGH WYCOMBE

Successive generations of Dashwoods have been trying to live down the exploits of the second Sir Francis who gained notoriety as a member of the Hell Fire Club. It is carefully pointed out these days that he was also Postmaster General from 1766 to 1781, a Fellow of the Royal Society and of the Society of Antiquaries, and a founder member of the Dilettanti Society. The second Sir Francis was also responsible for the transformation of West Wycombe House (built by his predecessor), continuing to make improvements until his death in 1781.

West Wycombe remains much as the second Sir Francis left it, and is acknowledged as an important monument to neo-classicism. Behind the façades, which include a double colonnade on the south front and a splendid Ionic portico on the west, are a series of rooms which continue the classical theme. The hall and staircase have been likened to a Roman atrium, the painted ceiling of the saloon represents the Council of the Gods, and that in the Blue Drawing Room, formerly the dining room, depicts the Triumph of Bacchus and Ariadne. Here also is a copy of the Venus de Medici. Much of the decoration is very rare, and is complemented with fine paintings and tapestries.

Open June to August afternoons, except Thursday and Friday. Tel: 01494 524411.

WEST WYCOMBE
Buckinghamshire

2 MILES (3 KM) NORTH-WEST OF HIGH WYCOMBE

The whole of West Wycombe is owned by the National Trust. In 1929 the Dashwood family put the house, park and village up for sale in 60 lots. The Royal Society of Arts, in a move to prevent the break-up of an estate village that had hardly changed since the 17th century, stepped in to buy the whole package. After sympathetic repair work, they handed it to the National Trust in 1934.

The village seen from the hill where Dashwood's mausoleum stands

By the time the Dashwood family acquired the estate of West Wycombe in 1698, the village had long since grown used to the traffic that passed through on the road from London to Oxford and beyond, and at the height of the coaching age there were eight coaching inns here. It was the activities of the second Sir Francis Dashwood in the 18th century, however, which really put the place on the map. Founder of the Society of Dilettanti and an altogether ravishingly eccentric character, he is notorious for his Hell Fire Club connections. It was he who had the Palladian house built and the park landscaped (by Humphry Repton), during the course of which he had the main road diverted from the village. The quarrying of chalk for the new road created the Caves, which were used for Hell Fire meetings. Above them is his folly of a mausoleum, and the church he had almost completely rebuilt to reflect his love of things Italian. In the golden ball on top of the tower, it is said, he held parties. The delightful village remains much as he inherited it. A few Georgian, brick or flint houses are interspersed between the small, timber-framed 16th-century houses. Arches lead into the courtyards of the old coaching inns, while Church Lane is entered beneath Church Loft, a medieval pilgrims' hospice.

This Victorian house has had a chequered history, and is now the headquarters of a religious sect

MENTMORE TOWERS
Buckinghamshire

6 MILES (9.5 KM) NORTH-EAST OF AYLESBURY

Mentmore Towers is certainly the kind of mansion one might expect to have been built for Baron Meyer Amschel de Rothschild at the height of the Victorian age of confidence and prosperity. It is a vast and splendid building in Elizabethan style, with huge windows and a many-turreted roofline, which was constructed in the mid-19th century to a design by Joseph Paxton and his future son-in-law, G H Stokes. Paxton was actually not a trained architect, but he was a great favourite of the Rothschild family, who were, perhaps, impressed by the Crystal Palace he had built for the Great Exhibition of 1851. Certainly, the building here makes great use of natural light.

Towards the end of the 19th century Mentmore became the home of Lord Rosebery, and was a glittering centre of social life for the wealthy and influential. It was also a veritable treasure-house of fine furniture and works of art and when, in the 1970s, the contents were put up for sale by auction there was a public outcry against the possible loss to the nation of important items. The auction went ahead, however, and raised over six million pounds in total. The building was subsequently purchased by the Maharishi Mahesh Yogi. It is still the headquarters of his University of Natural Law.

Open all year on Sunday and Bank Holiday afternoons. Tel: 01296 661881.

*The Moot Hall, once a
meeting-place for Bunyan's
followers*

ELSTOW
Bedfordshire

JUST SOUTH OF BEDFORD

Pilgrim's Start

'As I walked through the wilderness of this world, I lighted on a certain place, where was a den.' With these words John Bunyan began *The Pilgrim's Progress*. The settings for the story of Christian's journey towards salvation are often clearly based on places he knew locally. The 'den' is thought to refer to Bedford gaol.

*I*n 1660 Elstow's most famous son, John Bunyan, was taking part in the wrestling and dancing that took place on Sundays on the green, when he heard a voice from above asking 'Wilt thou leave thy sins and go to Heaven or have thy sins and go to Hell?'. Taking the first option, he became a Nonconformist preacher and thereby found himself in Bedford gaol. Here he stayed until 1672 and it was here, during another, shorter imprisonment, that he wrote The Pilgrim's Progress. Both this and Holy War are illustrated in stained glass in the church. The Norman church, a wonderful, lofty building with high arches and a large octagonal font where Bunyan and his daughters were baptised, is all that is left of a large nunnery. Once a year the nuns held a two-day fair, which gained a reputation for uproarious merry-making. Bunyan used it as the model for his 'Vanity Fair' and later Thackeray was to use it as the title of a novel. Attached to the church are the ruins of a 17th-century mansion. On the green the Moot Hall, a market hall dating from around 1500, houses a collection illustrating Bunyan's life and times. There are some fine black and white, timber-framed, overhung cottages, but Bunyan's humble tinker's home has long since gone.

FINCHINGFIELD
Essex

8 MIL:ES (13KM) NORTH-WEST OF BRAINTREE

The pond, the old brick bridge over the stream, the green with the church and a haphazard collection of cottages behind have somehow come together here to make a charming vignette, often featured on calendars. The attraction of this village lies in the delightfully unplanned manner in which the houses of differing sizes, styles and ages jostle together. Many have tiled roofs, some gabled, some with dormers, and many are plastered and colour-washed. Above the green, Finchingfield House has five barge-boarded gables, while the 18th-century coaching inn, The Fox, is pargeted. There is the red-brick Victorian school and the white Congregational chapel. The 17th-century house with four-stack chimneys by the footbridge was once the village workhouse and the timber-framed, white-gabled almshouses by the church, built in 1500 as the school, were later the guildhall. A passage leads through them to the church, standing up on the hill. Much of it is Norman, including the square west tower. The cupola replaces a spire which fell during a storm in 1702. Inside, look for the squares used in the medieval game of Nine Men's Morris, scratched on the south aisle window ledge. On the northern edge of the village is a white postmill and, near by, an unusual hexagonal thatched cottage stands.

One of the monuments inside the church is to William Kempe of nearby Spains Hall (d.1628) who, doing penance for falsely accusing his wife of infidelity, did not speak for seven years. For each year of his silence, it is said, he dug a pond in the grounds of his house.

The church towers ov er the jumble of rooftops.

❋

BETH CHATTO GARDENS
Essex

6 MILES (9.5 KM) EAST OF ELMSTEAD MARKET, COLCHESTER

❋

A perfect harmony of landscape and planting has been achieved by the water

No one who has seen Beth Chatto's display gardens at the Chelsea Flower Show can doubt that she is one of the most influential gardeners of our time, and a visit to her own gardens at Elmstead Market more than confirms this view. In her book *The Dry Garden*, Mrs Chatto emphasises that she selects each plant or tree 'for its shape and character, not for the colour of its flowers', and this respect for the habit of plants is the dominant impression you gain on entering the gardens.

Before 1960 there was neither house nor garden on the site, and with just a few trees in place, Mrs Chatto gradually converted the problem areas into gardens of different characters: the dry gravel parts are filled with drought-resistant plants bright with warm colours; a woodland garden lies in the shade of tall trees; and water gardens have been made where it was boggy before. These distinct types of garden now show an astonishing range of plants.

where a winding path meanders between lush shade-loving plants such as ferns, hostas, spotted pulmonarias and the elegant Solomon's seal, underplanted by the delicate purple-leaved violet.

Below, in a series of four pools surrounded by bog gardens, are some tall plants – angelicas, rodgersias, irises, the umbrella plant and bright yellow trollius. Bog arums and the

Initially, Mr and Mrs Chatto tackled the gravel areas which surround the house, and they constructed the Mediterranean Garden. The raised beds show bold contrasts of form and colour provided by plants like silver-leaved santolinas, artemisias, and variegated and purple-leaved sages. A Mount Etna broom with a fountain of tiny yellow, deliciously scented pea flowers dominates shrub planting of cistus, buddleia and many other species.

Leaving the warm Mediterranean Garden, there is a transformation in the cool grass beneath the tall oaks,

giant gunneras contrast with candelabra primulas, water forget-me-not, and *Pontederia cordata*, while, further away, but still enjoying the damp conditions, astilbes are underplanted with hostas. Where the pools narrow to a canal, bushes of *Viburnum plicatum* 'Mariesii' are loaded with white flowers in spring, while irises, ferns and New Zealand flax flourish in company with marsh marigolds, senecios · and pink polygonum.

Open from March to October, Monday to Saturday, and from November to February, Monday to Friday. Tel: 01206 822007.

Floral beds with hemerocalis, astilbes, delphiniums and filipendula curve away into the distance

LAYER MARNEY TOWER
Essex

6 MILES (9.5 KM) SOUTH-WEST OF COLCHESTER

When Henry VIII was on the throne, his namesake Henry, 1st Lord Marney, began to build a new home for himself which would reflect his new-found wealth and importance. He was a valued and respected member of the Privy Council under both Henry VII and Henry VIII, and his sound advice earned him first a knighthood and then a baronetcy. Though his great Tudor mansion was never completed, it remains as impressive today as when it was first constructed.

Layer Marney Tower, below, is a well-known East Anglian landmark, and the Long Gallery, right, was clearly conceived for entertaining on a grand scale

Layer Marney Tower, one of East Anglia's great landmarks and the tallest Tudor gatehouse in the country, has exceptionally fine brickwork and splendid terracotta decoration featuring shells and dolphins crowning the corner towers. The use of terracotta was a very recent innovation at that time, showing that Henry was seriously interested in keeping up with the trends of the times. Though there are actually only three storeys to the gatehouse itself, the hexagonal corner towers rise high above the roofline and have eight layers of windows. Between the corner turrets lie two respectably-sized rooms which may well have been used as state apartments for visiting royalty. Sadly, Henry Marney died before the building could be finished and his son died just two years later, leaving no-one to realise the dream.

Since that time the Tower has had a succession of owners, but each has admirably cared for this remarkable building.

East and west wings spread out on either side of the tower and there is a completely isolated south wing, not joined to the rest of the building at all, but these wings are all private living quarters of the owners and it is only the gatehouse that is open to the public. Visitors can climb right up to the top for a close look at the fine architectural features, and for good views, and there are displays of documents relating to the history of the tower and the families who have lived there over the centuries.

Within the grounds is a farm centred on a medieval barn and still worked by traditional methods. A farm walk takes in the variety of animals which are kept. Most of them are rare breeds, including Red Poll cattle and Norfolk Horn sheep, and there is a farming exhibition. Layer Marney had a licence to enclose deer in a park in 1267, and today there are 200 red deer again on the farm.

Open from April to September every afternoon, except Saturday. Tel: 01206 330784.

COLCHESTER CASTLE
Essex

COLCHESTER, 17 MILES (27.5 KM) SOUTH OF IPSWICH

Colchester is the largest Norman keep ever to have been built in Britain – larger even than the enormous Tower of London. Its dimensions are staggering –150 feet (46m) from north to south, 110 feet (34m) from east to west and as much as 110 feet (34m) high at its corner turrets. At their splayed bases, the walls are 17 feet (5.2m) thick, but taper slightly as they rise. Because it bears some similarities to the White Tower of London, some scholars believe that both were designed by Gandulf, Bishop of Rochester.

Colchester Castle, once known to the Saxons as King Coel's Palace, after the Old King Cole of the nursery rhyme

Unfortunately, the keep lost its upper storeys in the 17th century. There were originally four floors, but in 1683, the castle was sold to one John Wheeley, who wanted to pull it down and sell the stones. The great keep proved stronger than Wheeley had anticipated, and he gave up his demolition after the top two floors had proved something of a struggle. The idea of plundering ancient buildings arouses feelings of horror in these days of heritage conservation, but the castle itself was built from stones taken from nearby Roman ruins, and stands on the foundations of the Roman Temple of Claudius.

The castle now houses a museum, including archaeological finds from Colchester – the first capital of Roman Britain.

Open all year, daily, except Christmas. Tel: 01206 712931/712932.

HEDINGHAM CASTLE
Essex

CASTLE HEDINGHAM, 7 MILES (11 KM) SOUTH-WEST OF SUDBURY

Hedingham, like most Norman keeps, has its main entrance on the first, rather than the ground floor. This would have been accessed by a wooden staircase that could be pulled inside the castle in times of danger.

When the barons forced King John to sign the Magna Carta in 1215, they doubtless thought that it would bring an end to John's unpopular policies, but John was not bowed for long. Robert de Vere was the owner of Hedingham Castle, and among other of the barons who sided against their king, had his castle attacked twice in what became known as the Magna Carta Wars. John died soon afterwards, and Hedingham and other properties were restored to de Vere, whose family continued to own the castle until 1703.

Today, only the keep remains of the great 12th-century fortress, but it is one of the finest in England. The exact date that it was raised is not certain, but it was probably sometime between 1120 and 1140.

It has four storeys, although the second floor is double the height of the others. This second floor forms a magnificent hall, with elegant arched windows on two levels to provide plenty of light. The whole room is spanned by a vast Norman arch, and a gallery runs around the upper half of this splendid chamber.

Open from Easter to October, daily. Tel: 01787 60261.

The great keep of Hedingham Castle is one of the best preserved in Europe

A picturesque row of cottages
beneath the castle mound

PLESHEY
Essex

6 MILES (9.5 KM) NORTH-WEST OF CHELMSFORD

The whole of Pleshey village stands most evocatively within the earthworks of an important castle built in the 12th century by the Norman Geoffrey de Mandeville. Approach the village from the east, cross the outer bailey and the lane becomes the village high street. The vast, flat-topped mound can take one by surprise, rising up suddenly and dramatically behind the cottages, 60ft (18m) high and 300ft (91m) across at its base. The castle that stood on top was home for over 200 years to successive Lords High Constable of England before coming to Richard II's uncle, Thomas Duke of Gloucester. Gloucester founded a college of priests here in 1393 and the crossing arches of the building (but nothing else) are still to be seen within the church, extensively rebuilt in 1868. The only building preserved from the castle is the 15th-century brick bridge linking the mound with the inner bailey. It is said that, in 1558, when Queen Elizabeth's Commissioners discovered that the villagers were keeping rabbits in the castle ruins and this was their only means of access over the moat, they allowed it to remain. Walk across it on to the mound for wide-stretching views over the trees and attractive houses of the village to the farmlands of Essex.

THAXTED
Essex

7 MILES (11 KM) SOUTH-EAST OF SAFFRON WALDEN

Not only can Thaxted claim the most glorious church in Essex, it also boasts a most magnificent ancient guildhall. And, as if that were not enough, it has an uncommon wealth of other historic buildings. In the Middle Ages Thaxted became an important centre for the cutlery trade. There is no iron in the vicinity so it may have been that knives and swords were brought here for finishing. The guildhall, built by the cutlers in about 1400, stands at the centre of the village, a proud three-storey building, each floor overhanging the one below. All around it are more 15th-century timber-framed and overhanging buildings, some with pargeting. Other houses were medieval in origin and have Georgian plasterwork façades; a number date wholly from the Georgian period, by which time the cutlery trade had declined and Thaxted was a more modest market centre. All blend together most harmoniously. From the guildhall a narrow lane leads up to the church. Its spire soars over the buildings below in proclamation of the wealth of its medieval builders, the cutlers and the lords of the manor, the de Clares. There are some beautiful details externally, while the inside is light and airy. Near the church is a double row of almshouses, one thatched, with a view between them of Thaxted's disused tower windmill.

Gustav Holst, the composer, lived next to the Recorder's house in Town Street from 1917 to 1925, working mainly on comic operas and choral pieces.

The cutlers' guildhall with the church beyond

Among the many special features of Hampton Court is the enclosed Royal (or Real) Tennis Court

HAMPTON COURT
London

1½ MILES (2 KM) WEST OF KINGSTON-UPON-THAMES

The King's Court
Should have the excellence
But Hampton Court
Hath the pre-eminence
John Skelton (poet)

In Tudor times, the quickest and easiest route into London from Hampton Court was by river. The great astronomical clock in the Clock Court enabled Henry VIII to determine the times of high and low tide at London Bridge.

Nearly 600 years of history are contained within this vast royal palace on the Thames. In the early 16th century the lease was acquired by Cardinal Wolsey, Henry VIII's chief minister, and he added most of the Tudor buildings that we see today. They included a complete range of apartments for the use of Henry VIII, Catherine of Aragon and Princess Mary. When the Cardinal fell from grace in the 1520s the palace was handed over to Henry as a placatory gesture and the King added the Great Hall, with its wonderful hammer-beam ceiling, and vast kitchens to cater for his 1,000-strong retinue. Later monarchs all left their mark, too.

There is so much to see at Hampton Court that six separate routes have been devised, each exploring a different theme: Henry VIII's magnificent state apartments; the Queen's apartments, built by Sir Christopher Wren for Queen Mary; the elegant Georgian rooms; the King's apartments, built by William III and restored following a dreadful fire in 1986; the Wolsey Rooms, the earliest of the Tudor Rooms which now house important Renaissance paintings; and the Tudor kitchens, which occupy over 50 rooms and are set up as if in preparation for a great Tudor banquet. Some sixty acres (24ha) of gardens include the famous maze and the Great Vine.

Open all year daily, except Christmas and New Year's Day. Tel: 0181 781 9500.

HAM HOUSE
London

BETWEEN RICHMOND AND KINGSTON-UPON-THAMES

Ham house is an outstanding Stuart house which has managed to avoid the changes in architectural fashion that have altered so many of its contemporaries over the years. It was built in 1610 on the south bank of the Thames in the days when the river was the major thoroughfare into the city, giving its owner, Knight Marshall of the King's Household to James, essential access to the royal households.

Some 60 years later the house was enlarged and redecorated in the most fashionable style by the Duke and Duchess of Lauderdale, and much of their work is evident today. Even some of the furniture, specially made for the house in the 17th century, remains in situ. It is likely that we have the Duchess of Lauderdale's extravagance to thank because she left her descendant decidedly short of any funds which might have been used to make alterations. Even when the family fortunes took an upturn, they seemed loath to spend any money on the house and by the time it came into the ownership of the National Trust much restoration was necessary.

Today the interior decoration is again sumptuous, with painted ceilings, gilded plasterwork and rich colours, and there is a particularly fine library. The garden is also being restored to its original design.

Open April to mid-December on selected afternoons. Tel: 0181 940 1950.

Ham House is an example of fine restoration work by the National Trust

A delightfully impractical mansion in the classical style

CHISWICK HOUSE
London

BURLINGTON LANE, CHISWICK

Lord Burlington, who built Chiswick House in the 1720s, had a passion for the architecture of Ancient Rome, and his creation here is considered to be the finest classical building in the country. Regarded as fanciful and impractical by some of his contemporaries, Burlington's mansion is nevertheless an impressive manifestation both of his skill as an architect and his idealism.

The house is a square, two-storey structure with octagonal rooms at the centre – one above the other, surmounted by a shallow dome – and has two entrances. The modest ground floor entrance is completely overshadowed by the splendid, porticoed first-floor entrance, reached by grand flights of balustraded steps on either side. It is evident from this that the upper floor contained the principal rooms in which to receive guests and entertain friends. And it is thought that the house was always intended for entertainment – there are a number of bedrooms – but there was never a kitchen and meals were either taken in, or brought from the old house near by.

The interior of the house continues the classical style with themes taken from ancient Rome, and has intricately decorated painted ceilings, statues, columns and pedimented door frames.

Outside, the lovely Italianate gardens, with temples and statues, are being restored.

Open all year daily, but closed on Monday and Tuesday between October and March. Tel: 0181 995 0508.

KENSINGTON PALACE
London

KENSINGTON GARDENS, W8

In 1689, William III, who suffered badly from asthma, bought what was then called Nottingham House, the country home of the Earl of Nottingham. He employed Sir Christopher Wren to remodel it and moved the royal household from Whitehall to the cleaner country air of Kensington.

The palace was enlarged and redecorated again for George I and was the principal private residence of the royal family until the death of George II. Queen Victoria was born here, and it was at Kensington Palace, in 1837, that she learned of her accession to the throne at the age of 17.

The palace is now the London home of several members of the royal family, including the Prince of Wales, Princess Margaret, and Prince and Princess Michael of Kent.

The state apartments, with rooms by Wren and William Kent, are furnished with pieces from the royal collection, and other rooms are sumptuously decorated in classical 18th-century style, with wonderful painted ceilings and fine works of art, including a large number of royal portraits. The palace is also the home of the Royal Ceremonial Dress Collection which contains some of the magnificent costumes worn at Court from 1750 onwards, including dresses worn by Queen Victoria at all stages of her life.

Open all year daily, except certain Bank Holidays. Tel: 0171 937 9561.

Kensington Palace was once considered a country residence

The Tower is the scene of some historic ceremonies. Coronations and royal birthdays are celebrated by guns fired from the Tower, but perhaps more famous is the Ceremony of the Keys, carried out as the Tower is locked each night.

The Tower of London is one of the most outstanding examples of Norman architecture in Europe

TOWER OF LONDON
London

TOWER HILL, EC3

Standing proud and strong in the very heart of England's capital city, the Tower of London has had a long and eventful history. It conjours up many images for visitors – Beefeaters and ravens, the Crown Jewels, Traitors' Gate – and a multitude of executions.

William the Conqueror began work on the keep, known as the White Tower, in about 1078, but it was probably completed by William II some 20 years later. Building in the Tower of London complex has continued throughout history, right up to the Waterloo Barracks, built in 1845, and the brand new high-security jewel house. The variety of the buildings reflects the Tower's use as a royal residence, a prison, the Mint, the Royal Zoo, a public records office, the Royal Observatory and the stronghold for the crown jewels.

The Tower is noted for its bloody history. The first execution here is thought to have been that of Sir Simon Burley, who was beheaded in 1388. Two different places of execution are connected with the tower: Tower Hill, a patch of land outside the castle walls which was for public executions, and the more discreet Tower Green, inside the castle in the shadow of the White Tower. In 1465 a permanent scaffold was erected on Tower Hill by Edward IV. Countless heads followed the unfortunate Simon Burley's, including those of Sir Thomas More (1535),

Thomas Cromwell, the Earl of Essex (1540), and John Dudley, the Duke of Northumberland, and his son Guilford (1553). Tower Green witnessed the execution of two of Henry VIII's wives and the unlucky 16-year-old Lady Jane Grey, executed by 'Bloody Mary' in 1554.

Not everyone detained at the Tower was executed, and famous prisoners who languished within the gloomy walls included Princess Elizabeth (later Elizabeth I), Judge Jeffries and William Penn. But even when not under the threat of execution, prisoners were not necessarily safe. Henry VI was murdered in the Wake-

field Tower in 1471, and the boy king, Edward V and his brother, the Duke of York, are believed to have been murdered in the Bloody Tower. A number of prisoners attempted an escape – some successfully, like the charismatic Ranulf Flambard, Bishop of Durham, who climbed down a rope smuggled in to him in a jug of wine. Others were less fortunate – Gruffudd, the son of Llywelyn the Great, attempted a similar escape, but the rope broke as he climbed down it and he fell to his death.

Open all year, but closed Sundays between November and February, and at Christmas. Tel: 0171 709 0765.

Tradition has it that if the ravens ever leave the Tower, the monarchy will fall. Today, precautions are taken against such an event, including clipping the ravens' wings and keeping a number of extra ravens to hand.

OSTERLEY PARK
London

1 MILE (1.5 KM) NORTH-EAST OF HOUNSLOW

*T*he area between Heathrow Airport and Chiswick hardly seems a likely location for a splendid mansion set in 140 acres (56ha) of parkland, but this is where you will find Osterley Park. The original house dates back to 1575 when it was built for Sir Thomas Gresham, founder of the Royal Exchange, but it is actually known today as one of the most complete examples of the work of Robert Adam. Between 1760 and 1780 Adam transformed the house into a superb neo-classical villa, with the intricate plasterwork for which he was famous. By this time, Osterley was owned by Robert Child, a very wealthy London banker.

The house is entered by a huge double portico, built between the two towers of the original building, and this leads into a magnificent entrance hall with Roman statues and stucco panels. The state apartments include an ornately decorated four-poster bed, an ante room with Gobelin tapestries and a dressing room decorated in the Etruscan style, its walls ornamented with classical figures and urns. Adam's involvement at Osterley did not stop at the house – he also built the semi-circular garden house within the landscaped grounds.

A fine reminder of earlier times can be seen in the stable block which remains largely unaltered from Gresham's original building.

Open from April to October on most afternoons. Tel: 0181 560 3918.

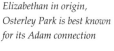
Elizabethan in origin, Osterley Park is best known for its Adam connection

WINDSOR CASTLE
Berkshire

WINDSOR, 2 MILES (3 KM) SOUTH OF SLOUGH

Windsor Castle is not only the official residence of HM The Queen, but also the largest inhabited castle in the world. The battlemented towers and turrets have been fortress, home and court to English monarchs since the 11th century.

William the Conqueror began work on the castle, raising a simple motte and bailey structure on a chalk cliff. Since then, Windsor has been almost continuously occupied, and many kings changed or added buildings during the next 900 years. Thus Henry II remodelled the great Round Tower, Edward III began to convert the military buildings into a royal residence, Edward IV started (and Henry VIII completed) the elegant St George's Chapel, and Henry VIII added the fine gatehouse. In the 1820s George IV spent a million pounds on modernising and repairing this splendid medieval fortress. The castle remained virtually unchanged from that time until the devastating fire in 1993, which destroyed parts of the historic buildings.

Windsor was a favourite among kings. Henry I was married here, Henry II planted a herb garden and regarded the castle as home, and Henry III famously entertained the local poor to a great feast here one Good Friday. Edward III was born in the castle, and his Knights of the Order of the Garter were later to adopt St George's Chapel as their place of worship. The castle withstood two sieges by King John during the Magna Carta Wars.

State apartments open all year, but subject to closure at short notice. Tel: 01753 831118.

Windsor is the largest inhabited castle in the world

THE MANOR HOUSE
Hampshire

UPTON GREY, 6 MILES (9.5 KM) SOUTH-EAST OF BASINGSTOKE

A few miles to the east of Basingstoke is one of the finest garden restorations of recent years. When Mr and Mrs J Wallinger came to the Manor House, Upton Grey, in 1984, the gardens were almost derelict, but as a result of careful research and meticulous and determined work, the layout and planting conceived by Gertrude Jekyll between 1908 and 1910 is now again beginning to provide a worthy setting for the house designed by that eminent country-house architect of the Edwardian period, Ernest Newton.

Although the yew hedging still has some way to go before it can again form the bones of the garden, Mrs Wallinger obtained all 15 Jekyll plans

paths wind their way between lilac and roses, such as 'Blush Rambler', 'Jersey Beauty', 'Kitchener of Khartoum' and 'Mme d'Arbelay', while hollies, laburnum, quince and medlar, weeping ash and walnuts give shape to the layout. In the beds leading to the pond, kniphofias, hemerocallis, irises and day lilies attract the eye, naturalised daffodils give a strong start to the season, and yew, bamboo and cotinus provide the background.

On the other side of the house a pergola stands between two formal borders planted with sedums, irises, anenomes, *Asphodelus lutea* and *Penstemon* 'Glaber', and steps lead down on to a grassy parterre. The

A pink rose cascades over the pergola, above steps leading to the parterre

dated 1908/9, followed her species and cultivars when she mentioned them in the planting plan for Upton Grey, and chose early varieties or those that Jekyll is known to have liked when she only mentioned the name of the species.

Perhaps even more exciting is the re-creation of the only Jekyll wild garden known to have survived, to the south-west of the house. Here, grass steps are being put back as an entrance to the garden, and sinuous

retaining walls are bright with rock roses, campanulas, aubretia and cerastrium, while the footing beds hold choisyas, eryngiums, rosemary and nepeta. In the parterre beds, lilies and cannas are surrounded by peonies, roses and stachys, while two further deep beds have a typically cool colour scheme, provided by *Santolina incana*, lady's mantle, lavender and rosemary.

Above the rose garden, lupins, rudbeckia, delphiniums and holly-

Lilies feature strongly in the design of this garden

hocks stand behind pale spiderwort, dwarf tritona and *Nepeta mussini*, and the herbaceous borders on the other side of the garden contain coreopsis, spirea and senecio in front of dahlias, asters and helianthus. The colours, too, are pale blues and yellows at the ends of the borders, rising to a climax of red *Papaver orientalis* and orange day lilies in the centre.

Open by appointment only. Tel: 01256 862827.

The sumptuous Victorian mansion of Highclere

HIGHCLERE CASTLE
Hampshire

5 MILES (8 KM) SOUTH OF NEWBURY

The 5th Earl of Carnarvon was fascinated by archaeology as a child and later spent every winter in Egypt. Though he helped to discover the tomb of Tutankhamun, and even looked inside it, he died before he could look upon the ancient king – some say he was the victim of a curse on the tomb.

Whether seen from a distance, from the approach through the park or from close quarters, Highclere Castle cannot fail to impress. It is hardly surprising that its architect, Sir Charles Barry, preferred it to the other building he was working on at the time – the Houses of Parliament. Highclere is a great square, honey-coloured building with a central square tower and an intricate roofline.

Inside, the castle is just as impressive, with a series of magnificent rooms, each with its own charm and character, from the Gothic, fan-vaulted entrance hall to the delicate boudoir, Lady Carnarvon's private sitting room.

Among the most magnificent rooms are the saloon, also Gothic and two storeys high, with an open gallery and splendidly rich decoration, and the huge double library, styled after the Reform Club library in London. The main staircase fills the great square tower at the centre of the house, while the drawing room, lined with family portraits, is in rococo revival style.

Highclere is the home of the Earls of Carnarvon, and it was the 5th Earl who, with Howard Carter, discovered the tomb of Tutankhamun. There is a display of excavated finds in the cellars.

Open daily from 4 May to September, except Monday. Tel: 01635 253210.

❈
BEAULIEU
Hampshire

BEAULIEU, 7 MILES (11.5 KM) SOUTH-EAST OF LYNDHURST

❈

Beaulieu is a comfortable mixture of ancient and modern

T he name of Beaulieu has become synonymous with the National Motor Museum, but behind all this is the lovely and very historic home of Lord Montagu. The house is part of the former Abbey of Beaulieu, the majority of which now forms a splendidly romantic ruin behind the house.

After Henry VIII dissolved the abbey in 1538, the square great gatehouse was converted into a home for the Wriothsley family. In the 18th century, Beaulieu passed by marriage to the family of the Dukes of Buccleuch, and the 5th Duke gave it as a wedding present to his second son, Lord Henry Scott, grandfather of the present Lord Montagu. He extended the house in Victorian Gothic style.

Today the family live in the Victorian wing, but the parts of the house which are on show are delightfully littered with mementoes of four generations. Ancestors gaze down from the walls of the picture gallery, and the entrance hall has objects reflecting the family's interests over the last 100 years.

When the house was enlarged and remodelled, many of the original features were retained and there are some wonderful vaulted ceilings. The family's coronation robes are displayed in the ante room, along with the velvet suit worn by Lord Montagu at the coronation of George VI and Queen Elizabeth.

Open all year daily, except Christmas Day. Tel: 01590 612345.

When Lord Montagu first opened his home to the public in 1952, five historic cars were positioned in the entrance hall to reflect his father's role as a pioneer motorist. That was the basis of what is now one of the finest motor museums in the world.

A view of the church, the courthouse and the village from the hill that was William of Wykeham's deer park

EAST MEON
Hampshire

5 MILES (8 KM) SOUTH-EAST OF PETERSFIELD

A model of the village as it must have looked in the days of the Normans was made for the Domesday 900th anniversary exhibition which was held in Winchester, where the *Domesday Book* was actually written. However, visitors must go to Normandy to see it now, where it is on permanent display in the Bayeux Tapestry museum.

When William the Conqueror ordered his Domesday survey in 1086, East Meon had for some time been an important settlement and the church that the Normans built here was conceived on a grand scale from the outset. Its main builder, Bishop Walkelin, also rebuilt Winchester Cathedral. This, the most exciting village church in the county, sits in a dominating position, right under the lee of a perfectly rounded, chalk downland hill, its elaborately decorated tower topped with a lead-covered broach spire. Within, the Romanesque arches of the 12th-century cruciform structure can easily be distinguished from the only significant addition, the 13th-century south aisle. Most precious is the black Tournai marble font brought over from Belgium in 1150 and boldly carved with the story of Adam and Eve. Probably it was a gift of Henry of Blois, a patron of artists and craftsmen and Bishop of Winchester at the time. The Bishops of Winchester were lords of the manor and their courthouse stands just below the church, built by William of Wykeham in 1395 as a hunting lodge. Forge Sound is a single-aisled house of 1350, and Tudor House has origins of similar date. Most of the other buildings of this quiet and unspoilt village, tile-hung or brick, with some flint and thatch, line the banks of the infant River Meon, beloved of Izaak Walton, author of *The Compleat Angler* (1653).

HAMBLEDON
Hampshire

8 MILES (13 KM) NORTH OF PORTSMOUTH

Manor Farm – this wing was added on at right angles to a medieval house

*I*t is as the 'cradle of cricket' that Hambledon will for ever be remembered. Cricket had been played for a long time before Hambledon Cricket Club was formed in about 1750, but within 20 years it had become the leading club in England and the chief authority for enforcing rules. Their moment of glory came in 1777 when, under Richard Nyren, the landlord of The Bat and Ball Inn on Broadhalfpenny Down, they beat an All England team by an innings and 168 runs. The village itself straggles along a valley bottom in wooded downland. There was a strong community here at the time of Domesday, and Henry III's granting of a licence for a weekly market in the 13th century was a boost to its prosperity. To this should be linked the extensive rebuilding of the church, incorporating into the nave the original, Saxon church. Markets continued to be held until the 17th century in the short but broad and pretty high street. In the main street Manor Farm is of particular interest, part of it being a stone, church-like 13th-century house. Some of the village houses have 16th-century origins hidden behind later façades, but most are Georgian brick, often painted, with tiled roofs and some use of flint. With inoffensive modern infill here and there, it adds up to an attractive village with a lively atmosphere.

*Then up with every glass and we'll
  sing a toast in chorus
The cricketers of Hambledon who
  played the game before us,
The stalwarts of the olden time
  who rolled a lonely down,
And made the king of games for
  men, with Hambledon the crown.*
Bruce Blunt, 'The Cricketers of
Hambledon' (1929)

The mellow golden stonework
of Stratfield Saye

STRATFIELD SAYE
Hampshire

6 MILES (9.5 KM) SOUTH OF READING

The Duke's charger,
Copenhagen, was buried in the
Ice House paddock where his
grave is marked with a
headstone and a turkey oak,
grown from an acorn planted
at the time of his burial.

A fter the Battle of Waterloo the first Duke of Wellington returned home a hero, and a grateful nation voted to grant him £600,000 with which to provide himself with a grand country house. He bought the estate at Stratfield Saye mainly for the parkland, for it was his intention to build a splendid new palace in the north-eastern corner.

Sadly, the grandiose plans for a palace to rival Blenheim far outstripped the joint funds of the national gift and his personal wealth.

Pragmatically, the Duke decided to settle for what he had, and set about modernising what was considered to be a modest house for so great a man. Among other improvements he installed blue patterned china water closets in every room and a central heating system – an unheard of luxury, and one which prompted Queen Victoria to complain that it was too hot. One of the original radiators can be seen in the staircase hall.

The main part of the house was built around 1630, and later additions,

including the conservatory and the two outer wings, have been carefully blended with the existing architecture.

If any room can be said to reflect its owner then it is the Hall, with its dignified, essentially masculine character and an array of items recalling Wellington's triumphs. There are paintings of events at Waterloo and the Peninsular War, busts of Wellington and Napoleon, and relics of the Duke's funeral.

The library has changed little since the 1st Duke's day and the music room is now dedicated to the memory of his favourite charger, Copenhagen, who carried him all day at the Battle of Waterloo. There are a number of paintings of the horse here and a bronze of Wellington mounted on him.

The tour of the house takes in many rooms, including the beautiful gallery, decorated in gold leaf, where there is a series of classical bronze busts. The charming 'small' drawing room, with French wallpaper, has a collection of miniatures, drawings and paintings, including a delightful study of the Duke and his grandchildren. The drawing room is a riot of green and gold with gilded plasterwork and Chippendale mirrors.

An exhibition on the life and times of the Duke of Wellington can be found in part of the stable block. This includes a special display relating to his state funeral, when a massive funeral carriage pulled by twelve dray horses was to process through London. In the event, the heavy carriage proved extremely difficult to manoevre.

Open from May to September daily, except Friday. Tel: 01256 882882.

SELBORNE
Hampshire

4 MILES (6.5 KM) SOUTH OF ALTON

Selborne was immortalised in 1789 by the publication of Reverend Gilbert White's *The Natural History and Antiquities of Selborne*. Since then his gentle, humorous and meticulous observations of life in the gardens, fields, hedgerows and woodlands around Selborne have become a favourite classic of country writing that has seen more than 200 editions. Gilbert White was born here in 1720, spent most of his life here as curate, and died in The Wakes in 1793, being buried in the churchyard. His gravestone is so simple it is easy to miss, bearing at his own request the plain inscription 'G W 26th June 1793'. Inside the church there is a window dedicated to him, alive with birds,

The village, seen from The Hanger

The Wakes, Gilbert White's home

Selborne, 9 September 1767
I was much entertained last summer with a tame bat, which would take flies out of a person's hand. If you gave it anything to eat, it brought its wings round before the mouth, hovering and hiding its head in the manner of birds of prey when they feed.

18 April 1768
The fly-catcher has not yet appeared: it usually breeds in my vine. The redstart begins to sing: its note is short and imperfect, but is continued till about the middle of June. The willow-wrens (the smaller sort) are horrid pests in a garden, destroying the pease, cherries, currants, etc.

1 August 1771
A neighbour of mine, who is said to have a nice ear, remarks that the owls about this village hoot in three different keys, in G flat, or F sharp, in B flat and A flat. He heard two hooting to each other, the one in A flat, and the other in B flat. Query: Do these different notes proceed from different species, or only from various individuals?

22 November 1777
This sudden summer-like heat was attended by many summer coincidences; for on those two days the thermometer rose to sixty-six in the shade; many species of insects revived and came forth; some bees swarmed in this neighbourhood; the old tortoise . . . awakened and came forth out of his dormitory.

(Observations from Gilbert White's *The Natural History . . . of Selborne*)

animals and flowers. There is also a beautiful Flemish 16th-century triptych depicting the Adoration of the Magi. Some alterations to the partly Norman, partly Perpendicular church were made in 1856 by Gilbert White's great nephew. Outside the church is the famous Selborne yew, 35ft (10.5m) in girth and nearly 1400 years old. In January 1990 it was blown down in a gale and split. It was replanted, having had its branches cut off, in the hopes that it will recover. Through the churchyard a path leads across watermeadows to the woods of Short Lythe and Long Lythe, National Trust land. Remains of a 13th-century Augustinian priory have been found near by.

Immediately adjoining the church-yard is The Plestor, the small village green, edged with old houses and sloping down to the road that goes right through the village. Near by, on this road, is The Wakes, White's home. Later it was the home of gallant Captain Oates, of Antarctic fame. The Wakes now houses a museum devoted to White and Oates. Behind the house is the garden Gilbert White so loved. On the other side of the road from the house can be seen the trees White planted to screen the blood and gore of the butcher's shop opposite. The houses and cottages along this, the main artery of the village, are mostly old and pleasant, brick and tiled, but not particularly distinguished.

Behind the Selborne Arms is the path that leads to the Zig-Zag, a path cut by Gilbert and his brother in 1753 that winds up the steep slope of The Hanger to the beechwoods and common at the top, also National Trust land. From the seat at the top there are far-reaching views over the rooftops of Selborne to the South Downs. Paths lead back down to the village.

Rhododendrons and azaleas colour the woodland without dominating it

SPINNERS
Hampshire

BOLDRE, 1 MILE (1.5 KM) NORTH-EAST OF LYMINGTON

Standing on a wooded slope falling westward towards the Lymington River, Spinners is a garden where the spirit of the New Forest has been jealously preserved. Although it is only 2 acres (1ha) in extent, it is full of interesting and beautiful plants, particularly those that like shady conditions. Part of the garden is sheltered by a canopy of oaks, but the layout also includes an open space and a fine lawn below the house. Numerous winding paths traverse the woodland, with glades charmingly opening up at intervals.

Rhododendrons and azaleas permeate but do not dominate the woodland. In spring a fine *Rhododendron Loderi* 'King George' shows its dark pink buds, while near by you can see *R. davidsonianum*, a triflorum with flowers that range

from pink to lilac-mauve. Camellias also feature – particularly the *williamsii* hybrids – as do magnolias and lacecap and mophead hydrangeas. There are a number of species of dogwoods, and Japanese maples are plentiful, especially the bright pink *Acer palmatum* 'Chisio Improved'. In spring the ground beneath the trees is thickly carpeted with flowers, including violets, periwinkles, erythroniums, anemones, bloodroot and lungwort. Later in the summer hostas and lilies take over, supported by euphorbias, particularly *E. griffithii* 'Fireglow'.

In a clearing below the steep woodland slope, fringed bleeding heart, with its blue-green leaves, is set against a berberis, while near by there are trilliums, hellebores and pulmonaria. Cranesbill geraniums are another speciality, and in a boggy area close by ostrich ferns and periwinkles flourish. The stone path that runs behind the house leads to an area with tree peonies, euphorbias, day lilies and lady's smock. Above the plant sales area there is a small path which runs among many varieties of erythroniums and passes a small example of *Rhododendron roxieanum orearastes*, which has glossy, narrow leaves and creamy flowers. To the south of the nursery is an open area where two outstanding magnolias can be seen, *Magnolia x loebneri* 'Leonard Messel', with lilac-pink flowers, and 'Merrill', which has white flowers. Although Spinners is a small garden, it has much to interest and delight the plant lover.

Open daily from mid-April to August, and by appointment. Tel: 01590 673347.

A wide variety of planting is packed into this small country garden, inluding many shade-lovers (left), and cranesbill geraniums (above)

Sunset and Evening Star
Many eminent Victorians were drawn to the Isle of Wight, among them the Poet Laureate, Alfred, Lord Tennyson, who had a house called Farringford there from the 1850s. He loved to stargaze through a telescope on his roof, walk on the down – which is now named after him – and contemplate the geology of Alum Bay. He wrote 'The Charge of the Light Brigade' and much of 'The Idylls of the King' there, entertained numerous distinguished visitors, and was made to pose for photographs by Julia Margaret Cameron, who lived at Dimbola near by. In 1888, after one of his last trips to the island on the Yarmouth ferry, he wrote 'Crossing the Bar'.

Sunset and evening star
And one clear call for me!
And may there be no moaning
*   of the bar*
When I put out to sea,

But such a tide as moving
*   seems asleep,*
Too full for sound and foam,
When that which drew from
*   out the boundless deep*
Turns again home.

ISLE OF WIGHT
Hampshire

The combination of sandy beaches and chalk cliffs topped by grassy downs helped to make the Isle of Wight a magnet to visitors in the 19th century. Among them were Queen Victoria, Prince Albert and their children, who had a summer holiday home near Cowes at Osborne House (English Heritage). Their presence helped to draw the middle-classes to the island, and the house was full of happy memories for the old queen when she died there in 1901. Though the island measures only 23 miles one way and 13 the other (37km and 21km), it has a surprising variety of scenery. At the extreme western tip, the Needles are pointed stacks of white chalk, surveyed cautiously from the mainland by the Needles Old Battery (National Trust), built in 1862 against the French. Nearby Alum Bay is known for its multi-coloured cliffs. There are said to be 12 different colours and shades of sand here (the main ones are yellow-brown, white, black, green and red) and they are used in souvenirs. To the east lie Tennyson Down (National Trust), where the poet liked to stroll, and the chalk cliffs of Freshwater Bay. The south-western coast is cut by a succession of deep chasms, or 'chines', penetrating inland – the best known

The sharp-tipped Needles were once joined to the mainland and the lighthouse was built in 1859

Above the sands at Ventnor, Victorian hotels and villas climb the steep Undercliff

and most commercialised of them is Blackgang Chine. A major factor in the 19th-century development of Wight tourism was the belief that the air and climate were good for invalids, and especially consumptives. The island's senior resort is sheltered Ventnor on the south-east coast, which at one time was officially declared to be the healthiest place in England. The seawall and esplanade were built in 1848 and eager developers piled Victorian Gothic and Seaside Swiss houses on the steep rock terraces of the Undercliff, with the front doors in one street lying level with the chimneys of another. A little to the north, Shanklin is another cliff-hanging Victorian and Edwardian resort, with a sandy beach that runs on to the amusements and mile-long esplanade of Sandown. Ryde, where the Portsmouth ferries arrive, is also popular with holidaymakers. Early August regularly brings Wight into the news as the yacht-racing season peaks at Cowes, where the Royal Yacht Squadron commands the harbour with a battery of miniature brass cannon. There is a good maritime museum here, and another at Bembridge, which has a fine natural harbour. Along the north-west coast, yachts and small craft proliferate among the narrow creeks.

A TICKET TO THE ISLE OF WIGHT

Newport

This is the capital of the Isle of Wight and its busiest town. A memorial to Princess Elizabeth, the second daughter of Charles I, can be found in the church. She died whilst in captivity in Carisbrooke Castle. The monument was commissioned by Queen Victoria. The town hall is by John Nash, who had a country retreat at nearby East Cowes Castle. A fine 3rd-century Roman villa in the town has brightly painted, reconstructed rooms.

Freshwater

Beloved by the poet Tennyson, who lived at Farringford (now a hotel). On the north side of Freshwater is Golden Hill Fort, a Victorian fortress with a pleasant sheltered courtyard and a variety of entertainments. The nearby Needles Pleasure Park is a must for children.

The place that claims to have more sunshine than anywhere else in England! This 72-mile (116km) drive takes you all round the island which in parts is quite unspoilt, a place of lofty downs with pretty thatched villages, set between the Solent and the English Channel.

➤➤➤➤

DIRECTIONS

Leave Newport by the A3020 (sp. Cowes) and in ¾ mile, at the roundabout, go straight on. In a further 2 miles, at Northwood, branch left on to the B3325 then in ½ mile bear right to skirt Cowes. After another ¾ mile, at the mini-roundabout, turn left, unclassified (no sign) and in ¼ mile go over the crossroads and descend Church Road. Shortly, turn right into Lower Church Road and, at the next T-junction, turn left (sp. Yarmouth) to pass Gurnard Bay. In 1¼ miles turn right at a roundabout and in a further 1½ miles bear right again (sp. Yarmouth) and continue to Porchfield. Continue and, in ½ mile, bear right, then in a further ½ mile turn right (sp. Newtown). Continue past the inlet of the Newton River and at the T-junction turn right (sp. Yarmouth). In ¾ mile, turn right

again on to the A3054 and enter Shalfleet. Follow signs to Freshwater and cross the Yar Bridge. Stay on the A3054 and continue through Colwell. Shortly, go forward on the B3322, Alum Bay road and enter Totland. At the roundabout bear right and enter Alum Bay. Return along the same road and in ½ mile pass the Museum of Clocks, then branch right, unclassified (sp. Freshwater Bay). In a further ½ mile, at the High Down Inn, bear right then turn left and continue to Freshwater and Freshwater Bay. Here, bear right to join the A3055 (no sign) and skirt Compton Bay. Continue along the coast road (sp. Ventnor) to reach Chale. Half a mile beyond the village, at the roundabout, take 2nd exit for Blackgang. Return to the roundabout and turn right with the A3055 (sp. Ventnor). Pass beneath St Catherine's Hill and continue to Niton. Here, keep left (one-way) then turn right. Continue through St Lawrence, pass the Undercliffe and Ventnor Botanic Gardens and proceed to Ventnor town centre. Leave on the A3055 (sp. Shanklin) and descend to Shanklin. Follow the main road through the town to Lake. Here, pass the Stag Inn and in ¼ mile at the war memorial, bear right. Pass beneath the railway and in just over ½

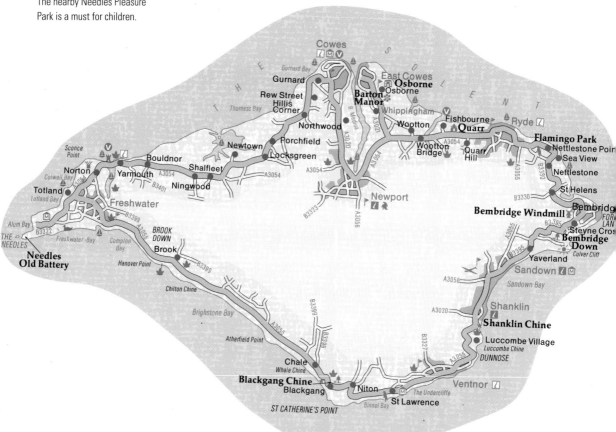

mile turn right (sp. Town Centre) to enter Sandown. Leave by the sea-front B3395 (sp. Bembridge) and in 1¼ miles, at the T-junction, turn right. Continue along the B3395 and in 1¼ miles pass Bembridge Airport. Bear left and after a further mile, at the mini-roundabout, turn left (unclassified) and continue to Bembridge. Follow the Ryde signs B3395 to skirt Bembridge Harbour, and at St Helens, at the T-junction, turn right on to the B3330 (sp. Nettlestone). In just over ¼ mile turn left (sp. Ryde) and continue to Nettlestone. Here, branch right on to the B3340 (sp. Seaview) and in almost ¼ mile further, branch right again, unclassified (sp. Sea Front). Continue to Seaview, descend the High Street, follow the Esplanade then keep forward into Bluett Avenue. At the T-junction turn right then keep left along the shoreline. Continue on the coast road, veer inland in ½ mile further turn right on to the B3330. Shortly, turn right again, with the A3055 then join the Esplanade to enter Ryde. Leave on the A3054 (sp. Newport) and after 1½ miles pass through Binstead. Continue to Wootten Bridge and in 1½miles, at the roundabout, turn right on to the A3021 (sp. East Cowes). In a further mile turn left (unclassified, sp. Royal Church of St Mildred), then in ½ mile pass the church at Whippingham. Continue to the T-junction and turn left into Victoria Grove. Join Adelaide Grove and at the end turn

right, on to the A3021 into East Cowes. Leave by the A3021 (sp. Newport, A3054). Continue on the A3021 and in ½ mile pass the road to Barton Manor Vineyard and Gardens on the left. In 1½ miles, at the roundabout, take 2nd exit A3054 and return to Newport.

>> ON THE TOUR >>

Cowes
Famous for Cowes Week, held in August, when thousands of yachtsmen – and landlubbers – flock to the town. The focal point is the Royal Yacht Squadron in West Cowes Castle, an exclusive gentleman's club founded in 1815.

Shanklin and Sandown
There is almost a continuous strip of seaside development here, with a cliff lift at Shanklin. The old village sits at the head of the chine. Keats came here for his health and stayed at what is now 76 High Street. Sandown is a mecca of seaside fun, with a zoo and a dinosaur 'museum'. It also has a fascinating Geology Museum.

Ryde
A large town that was once a small fishing village, Ryde is famous for its entertainments, its sandy beaches and its half-mile-long pier built in 1824, which made it possible to land from large vessels.

Alum Bay, famous for its multicoloured sands

Alum Bay and the Needles
The beach at Alum Bay is reached via a continuous chairlift. From the cliffs are dramatic views of the Needles, the famous chalk stacks.

The Undercliff and Ventnor
This part of the island was developed after 1829, when the physician Sir James Clarke recommended the area for those suffering from lung disease. The Undercliff is part of a complicated series of landslips on the Gault clay between St Catherine's Point and Ventnor. The lighthouse at the point is open at limited hours, subject to the fog signal not sounding.

OSBORNE HOUSE
Isle of Wight

1 MILE (1.5 KM) SOUTH-EAST OF EAST COWES

Queen Victoria and Prince Albert, dissatisfied with the turmoil of life at Court and the general lack of privacy they had to endure, decided to seek out a peaceful holiday retreat which would be large and private enough for their needs. Recalling happy childhood holidays, Victoria turned her attention to the Isle of Wight and in 1844 the royal couple rented Osborne House for a year's trial period. Though the original house proved to be too small, its situation on rising ground overlooking the Solent delighted the Queen and her consort and they bought the house and its 1,000 acres (405ha) of land in 1845.

Prince Albert remarked that the view from Osborne reminded him of the Bay of Naples, and when he and his builder, Thomas Cubitt, drew up plans for a new house it took the form of a Neapolitan villa, with Italianate campaniles and a loggia. The Prince, as keen on science and industry as he was on architecture, employed a number of innovative construction methods, including the use of cast-iron beams.

Outside, Albert created mock Renaissance terraces, with statues and a fountain, reaching down to the sea where they had a private beach, and planted acres of trees on the surrounding estate. He also imported a Swiss chalet as a play house for the royal children, but it had an educational purpose too – the boys were taught carpentry, the princesses learned cooking and household management, and each of the children had a garden plot where they grew flowers and vegetables.

This idyllic place became Victoria's favourite home and she lived here for most of the time until she died (at Osborne) in 1901. When Prince Albert died from typhoid in 1861, the heartbroken queen issued instructions that

Osborne was designed in the style of an Italianate villa, below, with right, matching terraces and gardens

nothing at Osborne should be changed so that it would remain as a memorial to the man who had created it. Hardly anything has changed here since Queen Victoria died either, and there are many of her personal possessions, including her own and Prince Albert's paintings and gifts among the grand works of art and statues which adorn the state rooms.

In contrast to the Italian style, the Durbar Room, added in 1891 as a dining room and decorated in Indian style by Indian craftsmen, reflects the Queen's role as Empress of India.

Osborne is now not only a memorial to Prince Albert, but also to his remarkable Queen and to the Victorian age.

Open from April to October daily. Tel: 01983 200022.

In her memoirs Queen Victoria noted that she and Prince Albert would often walk in the woods at Osborne and that Albert would imitate the distinctive song of the nightingale, his favourite bird – frequently receiving a reply.

ISLE OF WIGHT STEAM RAILWAY

Isle of Wight

SMALLBROOK JUNCTION, 1½ MILES (2.5 KM) SOUTH OF RYDE

Havenstreet station, a busy place with a museum about the island's railways as an added attraction

*Q*ueen Victoria popularised the Isle of Wight with her purchase of Osborne House and subsequent regular visits, and the island was once served by a characterful and extensive railway network. It was entirely worked by tank locomotives and, before the motor car eroded its traffic, carried huge numbers of holidaymakers.

The two lines that remain open could hardly be more different from each other, but they are linked by an interchange station, and the Ryde–Shanklin line, still part of the national railway system, is the best way to reach the Isle of Wight Steam Railway. First-time visitors from London to the island are often surprised by the train awaiting them as they step off the Wightlink ferry from Portsmouth at Ryde Pier – the last

thing they would expect to see here is Piccadilly line stock. Much of it was over 30 years old when it was brought across the Solent in 1966, so it conveys something of a museum feel to what is an excellent service. From Ryde it is a short journey to Smallbrook Junction where in 1991 Network SouthEast built a new station to serve the preserved steam railway. Anyone who recalls the days of steam on *Vectis*, as the Romans called the island, would recognise most of the locomotives and carriages that run to Wooton, the western terminus of the 5-mile (8km) line.

It is one of the particular pleasures of the Isle of Wight Steam Railway that almost all its carriages were built before World War I, and the standard of restoration is quite exceptional. Often passengers spend the first mile or two of a journey admiring the

interior of their carriage, rather than enjoying the scenery. The first part of the line, to the railway's headquarters at Havenstreet, is through woodland carpeted in bluebells in May followed by views across fields to distant hills.

It is well worth stopping off at Havenstreet to look at the museum about the island's railways, situated beside the shop in a former gasworks building. Rather surprising for a rural location, this structure was built as an act of benevolence by local landowner John Rylands, well-known to Mancunians for the library named after him. The engine shed can also be visited under supervision. The activity at Havenstreet today is a marked contrast to the peace of earlier times, when the tranquillity induced adders and a swan to find their way into the ground-level signal box – though not at the same time.

Train service: from mid-July to early September, daily except Saturdays. Tel: 01983 882204.

Still going strong – London Brighton & South Coast Railway 0-6-0T No 11 was built in 1878, one of the famous 'Terrier' AIX class

CARISBROOKE CASTLE
Isle of Wight

CARISBROOKE, JUST SOUTH-WEST OF NEWPORT

While a prisoner in Carisbrooke Castle in the summer of 1647, Charles I claimed to his startled supporters that he could escape from his prison because he had tested the size of the bars on the window against his head. What his head could pass through, the rest of his body, he assured his friends, could follow. After some undignified struggling, Charles was forced to admit that he had misjudged. Unfortunately for Charles, this was not his only error of judgement, and he was executed in London some 18 months later.

A mound was built here in about 1070, four years after the Battle of Hastings, and a stone shell keep was built on the mound 70 years later. In the 14th century, England feared an attack by the French, and it was at this time that the spectacular gatehouse was built. The French did actually manage to land on the island, but the castle was not attacked.

In the 1580s, it was the Spanish who threatened invasion, and the castle was altered and adapted so that it would be able to repel an attack by guns. There are several buildings in the castle courtyard, one of which houses a museum, another the well house.

Open all year daily, except at Christmas and New Year. Tel: 01983 522107.

Carisbrooke is the island's only remaining medieval castle

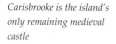

PORTCHESTER CASTLE
Hampshire

4 MILES (6 KM) EAST OF FAREHAM

The origins of Portchester castle stretch much further back in time than its Norman buildings, for Portchester was a Roman coastal fortress constructed in the 3rd century AD. The Roman walls still stand tall and strong today, as they did when the Normans came and built a great keep inside this sturdy fortress.

The Roman fort was a great square enclosure, protected by high walls studded with protective towers. In 1120 the Normans built a fine keep using cut stone imported from Caen in France. Originally the keep was only two storeys high, but about 50 years later it was given an additional two floors, and 200 years after this, Richard II added battlements.

Because of its strategically important position on the coast, several medieval kings spent a good deal of money on maintaining and improving the castle. Richard II is believed to have raised the buildings between the keep and the gatehouse called 'Richard's Palace'. Edward I presented the castle first to his mother and then to his wife. Before the castle came into royal hands, Augustinian Canons built a priory in the south-eastern corner of the fort, and their splendid chapel can still be seen by visitors to the castle.

Open all year daily, except Christmas and New Year. Tel: 01705 378291.

Left to fall into disrepair, only parts of Portchester Castle remain today

GODSHILL
Isle of Wight

3 MILES (5 KM) WEST OF SHANKLIN

In the summer months Godshill's high street buzzes with visitors swarming around a cluster of 'attractions' that few other villages in Britain can hope to compete with. There are two toy museums, a natural history centre, a model village and gardens, all served by tea-rooms and a pub. Just up the hill, however, as though standing a little aloof from all this tacky tourism, is the original, picture postcard Godshill. A perfect group of neat, thatched, greyish-stone cottages nestles under the tower of the 15th-century church: not without reason did this become a show village, but the cost of commercialism is dear.

The church, which celebrated its 950th anniversary in 1992, is not the first to stand on top of this, God's hill, overlooking the south of the island. The story goes that when the Saxons were preparing to build a church a mile or so away, their stones were miraculously moved in the night to the top of this hill. Taking this as an omen, they built their church here instead. The base of the present tower dates from the 14th century but the pinnacled top is 16th-century. Some of the windows and the transepts are also 14th-century, one with a plastered wagon roof from the 15th century. But what is very special is the painting – and one wonders how many of Godshill's visitors venture up to the church to see this jewel. In the south transept is a medieval wall painting depicting Christ crucified on three leafy branches of a flowering lily. The extent of the naturalism is rare in so early a painting, and the mural is said by some to be unique in Britain. Also of interest is a large painting of Daniel in the lions' den, by Rubens or his school, that came from nearby Appuldurcombe House, seat of the Worsleys. Many of the effigies are to members of that family.

Several of the old houses in the village are stone-built and a number still have their thatched roofs. There is the stone 1826 school and a Wesleyan chapel of the 1840s. The Griffin Hotel is an attractive building, with bargeboarded gables. The Old Smithy does good trade, though no longer from blacksmithing, while the old vicarage gardens house the model village with its 1:10 scale replica of the church standing in the shadow of the real thing. So faithful a reproduction of the village is the model, that it incorporates a model of itself, a model of a model village.

The history of Godshill is linked closely to Appuldurcombe House, a Palladian-style mansion whose ruined shell can be visited a mile south. It was built in the early 1700s by Robert Worsley, whose family had long since been influential in the island. A later owner, Lord Yarborough, built the schoolhouse in the village, as well as The Griffin pub whose sign depicts the Worsley family insignia.

The church and cottages of the real Godshill, left can be seen faithfully reproduced in miniature, below

NEW NATIONAL PARKS

A New Forest pony and foal graze peacefully, in a scene typical of Britain's latest proposed National Park

*I*f there's one thing that the New Forest – the latest area to be granted the status of a National Park – is not, it's 'new'. Most National Park designations date from the 1950s, but the one notable exception is the New Forest which was 'designated' in AD1079, when William the Conqueror first set aside, with a strict set of laws for the protection of game, what he called his 'Nova Foresta'.

The 145 square miles (376 sq km) between Southampton Water and Salisbury Plain merited two full pages in William's famous Domesday survey and the miracle is that, nine centuries later, the description of infertile woodland and furzy waste where William of Normandy hunted his beloved deer still holds true today.

The New Forest has been described as the largest area of uncultivated lowland landscape in North-West Europe, and is still mostly Crown property, administered by the Forestry Commission. The Commission's enlightened policies, especially with regard to the 'Ancient and Ornamental' woodlands, has done much to safeguard this amazing remnant of medieval greenwood: the commons are administered by the ancient New Forest Verderers.

This commendable record of forest management must have influenced the Government in its recent announcement which gave the New Forest the equivalent status of a National Park. Administered by a re-formed Heritage Area Committee, and jointly funded by local and central Government, the new body will have the same responsibilities as a National Park authority, but without its control over development, and planning powers. For many conservationists this is unsatisfactory, and the Council for National Parks has repeated the call for real National Park status to be conferred on the New Forest. However, John Dower would not have excluded the New Forest in his priority list for National Parks in 1945 had he not been reasonably satisfied that it was already in safe hands with the Forestry Commission. He attached the same kind of proviso to the South Downs, where he thought the local authorities would make adequate provision for conservation and recreation. Nevertheless, although the South Downs of East and West Sussex are already an Area of Outstanding Natural Beauty, local authorities in the area have mounted a vigorous campaign for National Park status. It could be argued that areas like the Downs are under the greatest pressure, not only from development and recreation, but from widespread agricultural 'improvement', although the withdrawal of cereal subsidies from Europe has eased the threat to the precious downland that remains.

Apart from the Broads, our present National Parks are mostly of an upland character, largely because the original definition of a National Park referred to 'relatively wild' country and because, generally speaking, less harmful change has taken place in the uplands.

To redress the balance, however, further lowland National Parks have been suggested over the years. These include the Somerset Levels, still threatened by agricultural drainage schemes; the sylvan Wye valley; the beech-hung Chiltern Hills; the Shropshire Hills; and the rolling, honey-stoned Cotswold Hills, one of the largest existing AONBs.

Where the South Downs meet the sea – the Seven Sisters, near Seaford

LITTLE GADDESDEN
Hertfordshire

6 MILES (9.5 KM) NORTH-WEST OF HEMEL HEMPSTEAD

*L*ittle Gaddesden lies on the Bedfordshire/Buckinghamshire border, deep in the woodlands and commons of the Chiltern Hills and bordering on the vast parklands of Ashridge House. Ashridge was originally built as a College of Bonshommes by the Normans but was suppressed at the dissolution and subsequently sold. It remained in the possession of the Earls of Bridgewater until bought by the National Trust in 1947. In 1808 Ashridge was rebuilt by James and Jeffry Wyatt on a colossal scale, in sumptuous Gothic Revival style. Little Gaddesden dates mainly from the 16th century when the monastic buildings were turned into a large house at the centre of a huge estate. A 'B' and a coronet can be seen on many of the houses, showing that they were estate workers' cottages. The village is basically one street, with houses and cottages straggling along one side only, set back from the road behind a broad stretch of grass. John O'Gaddesden's House, named after the 14th-century royal physician, is a delightful timber-framed, pargeted house of the 15th century. The stone-built manor house, dated 1576, has two turrets with stepped gables. The village church, interesting only for its monuments, is half a mile away from the houses. Its isolation, together with the existence of various humps and bumps near by, suggest a deserted village.

Timber-framed Manor Cottage

Memorial
The Ashridge Estate covers some 4000 acres (1620ha) of woodlands and commons and is open to the public. A focal point is the granite monument erected in the middle of the 19th century to the 3rd Duke of Bridgewater, the 'Canal Duke', who commissioned James Brindley to build England's first canal from his Worsley coal mines to Manchester. It opened in 1761.

'You know very well that when the health, life and beauty now overflowing these halls shall have fled, crowds of people will come to see the place where he lived and wrote.'
Charles Dickens, making a speech in Knebworth's Banqueting Hall in which he referred to his friend and host Sir Edward Bulwer-Lytton

The elaborate Gothic banqueting hall

KNEBWORTH HOUSE
Hertfordshire

STEVENAGE, WITH DIRECT ACCESS OFF THE A1(M) AT JUNCTION 7

Successive owners of Knebworth House have been unable to resist wielding the hand of change. It was built by Sir Robert Lytton in 1490 and for about 300 years developed and grew until Mrs Elizabeth Bulwer-Lytton demolished a large part of it in 1810. It was her son, the Victorian author and playwright Sir Edward Bulwer-Lytton, who transformed the house into the vision of unrestrained High Gothic splendour we see today. It is theatrical and romantic, its roof line a mass of battlements, turrets and heraldic beasts.

Inside is a series of magnificent rooms – the banqueting hall, a fine example of 17th-century architecture; the elegant dining parlour; the richly decorated library; the ornately Victorian state drawing room; the charming Regency bedroom of Mrs Bulwer-Lytton and the Tudor-style Queen Elizabeth Room.

Bulwer-Lytton's study recalls the life and work of the author and there is an Indian exhibition – Robert, 1st Earl of Lytton was the Viceroy who proclaimed Queen Victoria Empress of India. All around are family portraits and photographs, and the Hampden Room contains the family collection of children's furniture, toys and books.

Open at Easter, and from June to August daily, except Monday, weekends and Bank Holidays in April, May and September. Tel: 01438 812661.

HATFIELD HOUSE
Hertfordshire

HATFIELD

The spacious Privy Garden, surrounded by a walkway of pleached limes

Both setting and history combine to make the gardens of Hatfield House one of the most outstanding in the country. The Jacobean house was built between 1607 and 1611 by Robert Cecil, chief minister to King James 1, and this mellow brick building, together with the remaining great hall wing of the Old Palace of Hatfield, where Princess Elizabeth was confined during her sister Mary's reign, provide the backdrop for gardens that were planned by John Tradescant the Elder. Today, the gardens are fortunate in that the present Marchioness of Salisbury has set herself the task of remaking the layout as it might have been during Stuart times.

From the north court of the great house you pass directly into the West Gardens and to a border planted with yew and *Phillyrea latifolia*. Approaching the deep-red façade of

the old Palace, you look down on to the knot garden in the manner in which it might have been seen in the 17th century. The seven knots of the garden were made by Lady Salisbury in the 1980s, following an Italian design, with the outer hedges of clipped hawthorn incorporating seats over which honeysuckle has been trained. The knot hedges themselves are of box with small cones at the corners, and are filled with spring bulbs that are succeeded by flowering plants and shrubs later in the season. Crown imperials, tulips, anenomes and violets bloom here in the spring, beside hellebores and the blossom of both almond and cherry trees, while in summer shrub roses contrast in shape and colour with delphiniums and pinks.

Yew hedges border the Privy Garden, and there is a pleached lime walk on all four sides. In springtime

The beautiful knot garden incorporates a maze

the beds are filled with tulips, wallflowers and polyanthus in contrast to euphorbias and hellebores. Later, peonies and mauve and red penstemons come into flower, and old shrub roses give height to the planting. Further on you descend into the scented garden, with walks between beds of camomile, lavender and thyme, and a herb garden with a central sundial. A beautiful wisteria hangs over a seat, and there are also several varieties of philadelphus, winter sweet and a fine *Mahonia japonica* to be seen.

A gate leads you into a wilderness, with winding paths through woodland that includes a Spanish chestnut (possibly dating from the 17th century), golden elms, silver birch and amelanchier. In spring this wonderful area shines with rhododendrons, camellias and magnolias underplanted with crocuses and lily of the valley. For the intrepid visitor, there are still the East Gardens to see, with a spectacular parterre, a maze, a pool garden and an orchard. Hatfield House gardens combine a magnificent historical layout with modern plantsmanship of the very highest standard.

Open daily, from late March to October. Tel: 01707 262823.

An inviting gate leads from the scented garden to the 13 acres (5ha) of wilderness

BENINGTON LORDSHIP
Hertfordshire

BENINGTON, 4 MILES (6.5 KM) EAST OF STEVENAGE

A brilliant show of colour in the deep herbaceous borders

Benington Lordship is one of those rare gardens which has almost all the advantages. Situated near Stevenage, it occupies a site that has been inhabited since the Norman Conquest, and can boast a keep which dates from the 11th century, a moat which is covered with snowdrops in early spring, fine views over the surrounding countryside, a colourful rockery and large herbaceous borders.

In 1905, when the present owner's grandfather, Arthur Bott, bought the property, there was no garden, and the area now occupied by the park and garden was a nine-hole golf course. As well as enlarging the house,

Mr Bott created a garden with a characteristic Edwardian flavour which is still maintained by Mr and Mrs C H A Bott and their head gardener, Ian Billot. Benington Lordship stands 400 feet (122m) above sea level on heavy clay, so that the beds have to be heavily mulched with compost and manure. Much of the grass is not cut until the full summer, and in consequence the gardens are famous for their spring colour, with drifts of snowdrops, scillas, cowslips and garlic.

In front of the house, the Rose Garden has been replanted with the fragrant, bluish-white rose 'Margaret Merril' and with 'Radox

Bouquet'. Along the verandah, which recalls Arthur Bott's time in India, is a collection of yellow shrub roses, including 'Agnes', the fragrant *Rosa primula*, the incense rose, and 'Fruhlingsdrift'. From the west end of the house there are splendid views over the old entrance drive, and a large urn, found in the moat, has been surrounded by a camomile lawn and by *Rosa moyesii* 'Geranium'. Beyond the urn, a path leads into the moat, past a number of crab apple trees and cowslip and heather banks.

The rockery was planned during World War I around a spring in the top pool, and now, once the early bulbs are over, it displays attractive groups of primulas, herbs and alliums.

Set surprisingly far away from the house, two wonderfully deep borders run east to west below the kitchen garden and plant centre. Interrupted by fine, brick gate-piers, the borders are bright in summer with rock roses, sedums, salvias and potentillas. At Benington Lordship, the kitchen garden still grows vegetables, while, backing on to the herbaceous border are beds full of the most wonderful autumn colour, one overflowing with Michaelmas daisies – so popular a plant during Edwardian times.

Open from April to September, on selected afternoons. Tel: 01438 869668.

This curious figure of Shylock emerges from a sea of white 'Iceberg' roses

BLENHEIM PALACE
Oxfordshire

WOODSTOCK, 8 MILES (13 KM) NORTH-WEST OF OXFORD

'We have nothing to equal this.'
George III

Below and right, Blenheim is one of the great palaces of Britain

This is one of Britain's grandest palaces, an enormous Italianate edifice which covers seven acres (2.8ha) of ground. Between them, the original architect, Vanbrugh, and landscape artist 'Capability' Brown have created breathtaking sights at every turn, from the first glimpse of the palace through the entrance arch to the splendid vista across the lake and its classical Grand Bridge.

The estate and the cost of building the palace was the gift of a grateful Queen Anne to the heroic Duke of Marlborough in thanks for his victory at the Battle of Blenheim. The Duke and his Duchess, Sarah, had long been close friends of the Queen and at the time there seemed no bounds to the monarch's generosity. However, the Duchess later quarrelled with the Queen, lost her place at Court, and royal contributions to the cost of building Blenheim ceased. The Marlboroughs retreated abroad, returning only after the death of Queen Anne to finish Blenheim at their own expense. The path was still not a smooth one, though, for the Duchess also quarrelled with the architect! None of this detracted from the end result, and successive Dukes of Marlborough have maintained and contributed to its grandeur and its wonderful art collection.

Within the house is a stunning series of rooms of magnificent proportions, with rich decoration and many splendid painted ceilings by Louis Laguerre and Sir James Thornhill. There are works of art by Reynolds,

Van Dyck and Kneller, wonderful wood carving by Grinling Gibbons and fine tapestries. The most famous tapestry, in the Green Writing Room, depicts the 1st Duke of Marlborough accepting the surrender at Blenheim. The saloon, which is, in fact, the state dining room, is sumptuously decorated, with ceiling and wall paintings by Laguerre and marble doorframes surmounted by crests. The table is laid with a Minton dinner service, and there is a silver centrepiece of Marlborough on horseback. Connecting with the saloon are three more state rooms, all hung with tapestries of Marlborough's campaigns.

In contrast, many visitors to Blenheim are delighted by the modest little room in which Sir Winston Churchill was born in 1874 (Churchill is the family name of the Dukes of Marlborough, and Sir Winston was cousin to the 9th Duke). Within the 2,100 acres (850ha) of grounds are beautiful formal gardens which have been likened to those at Versailles, an arboretum and a walled garden containing a maze, kitchen gardens and an adventure playground.

Open from mid-March to October daily. Tel: 01993 811091 or 811325 (information line).

In 1988 Blenheim Palace became the fourth site in the United Kingdom to warrant inclusion in the World Heritage List.

Above, swans are the perfect ornament on the moat of this lovely medieval manor house, and right, boxed hedges make an unusual design in the old walled garden

BROUGHTON CASTLE
Oxfordshire

BROUGHTON, 3 MILES (5 KM) SOUTH-WEST OF BANBURY

On a fine summer day, with its golden stone walls reflected in the waters of its moat, it would be hard to find a more picturesque sight than Broughton Castle. It is, in reality, not a castle at all but a splendid medieval manor and most of the original house remains today. There was already a house on the site when Sir John de Broughton built his manor in 1300; then, in the 16th century, it was extended and altered, transforming Broughton into a fine Tudor home. Today, the Great Hall is a curious mixture of medieval stone walls, 16th-century windows and an 18th-century plastered ceiling, and with its suits of armour and an unusual collection of leather buckets it has enormous charm and character.

The oldest part of the house is represented in the groined passage and in the dining room, which was an undercroft in the Middle Ages. There are old stone passageways with vaulted ceilings and grotesque corbel heads at the base of the arches, and a spiral staircase. Another staircase leads to the rare 14th-century chapel with a traceried window, heraldic glass and a fixed stone altar.

The character of the house changes completely in the charming Queen Anne's Room, named to commemorate

a visit by Queen Anne of Denmark, wife of James I, in 1604. It is a light and sunny room with a pretty 18th-century four-poster bed and a splendid fireplace. The King's Chamber, used by both James I and Edward VII, has a remarkable stucco overmantel dating from 1554, and Chinese hand-painted wallpaper. The Oak Room is pure Tudor, with floor-to-ceiling oak panelling and an unusual interior porch, and the gallery has a series of family portraits. The family in question are the Fiennes, Lords Saye and Sele – the present Lord is the 21st Baron – and their lineage can be traced on the family tree in the Great Hall.

William Fiennes was a prominent Parliamentarian during the Civil War, refusing to take the Oath of Allegiance and hosting meetings at Broughton to plan Parliament's opposition to Charles I. He disapproved of the execution of the King, however, and removed himself from public life, an act which earned him a pardon on the Restoration in 1660. Another notable member of the family was Celia Fiennes, remembered for her journals documenting her extensive travels around England at the end of the 17th century.

Open over Easter, then from mid-May to mid-September on selected days. Tel: 01295 262624.

GREAT TEW
Oxfordshire

6 MILES (9.5 KM) EAST OF CHIPPING NORTON

*H*ere is a rare place. It was a work of art, a planned estate village that was the epitome of the perfect English village; but so dilapidated did it become that in 1978, in an effort to save it from total decay, it was declared a conservation area. Lucius Cary, Lord Falkland, lived here in the 17th century entertaining philosophers and poets, and built many of the cottages that still stand today. In 1808 J C Loudon was given free reign by General Stratton to prove his theory that beauty and utility are not incompatible in wholescale landscape improvement. He was against the idea, in vogue at the time, of removing any existing village out of sight and sound of the new big house, considering that the cottages and their gardens were actually an enhancement. All around the 14th-century church, the manor house, the thatched or stone-roofed cottages, the Victorian school, the pub and the green with its stocks are the evergreen trees that Loudon planted to show off to its best the rich colour of the limestone. The recent restoration work means that few cottages are now totally derelict, but with this rejuvenation has inevitably come a change of character, a loss of a certain charm. Cottages are smartened up, gardens are suburbanised, weekenders have arrived – but the village of Great Tew is brought back from near oblivion.

The characteristic rich ocre of the stone, here set off by neat thatch

KINGSTON BAGPUIZE HOUSE

Oxfordshire

KINGSTON BAGPUIZE, 5 MILES (8 KM) WEST OF ABINGDON

Lady Tweedsmuir's father-in-law was the writer John Buchan, 1st Baron Tweedsmuir,. He wrote historical works as well as better-known adventure stories such as *The Thirty-nine Steps.*

No-one knows for certain when Kingston Bagpuize House was built, but it is thought to date from around 1670. It is a charming place, with a distinct 'lived-in' character.

One of its most important architectural features is the splendid cantilevered staircase, which has no supporting pillars. The pine-panelled hall and staircase have a Chinese theme, with hand-painted Chinese wallpapers and antique vases. The saloon is central to the whole design of the house – all the principal ground floor rooms can be seen from here, and the door into the garden was once the main entrance to the house. The further rooms are again panelled, with either oak or pine, and are beautifully furnished.

Originally the first floor had a great chamber, but this was divided up, probably in the early 18th century. The Rose Bedroom occupies some of this space, while the adjoining Lady Tweedsmuir's Bedroom would formerly have been the withdrawing room. Both have four-poster beds and fine Georgian furniture.

Today's visitors can take tea in the old kitchen, which has been very little changed to accommodate this facility, retaining its old dresser with kitchen china, a fine array of copper pans and a knife sharpener. The beautiful gardens were created by Miss Marnie Raphael, who lived here from 1939 to 1976 and was the aunt of Lady Tweedsmuir, the present owner.

Open for 30 days a year during the summer. Tel: 01865 820259.

This charming home has the perfect proportions of a doll's house

HASCOMBE COURT
Surrey

2½ MILES (4 KM) SOUTH-EAST OF GODALMING

Broad herbaceous borders lead up to the splendidly overgrown summerhouse

Situated to the south of Godalming, Hascombe Court nestles deep in the lush Surrey countryside. The extensive gardens were originally designed by Gertrude Jekyll, and remodelled in 1928 and 1929 to enable the front entrance to the house to be properly visible. During the past 12 years, the present owners, Mr and Mrs O Poulsen, have carefully restored the layout after a period of decline.

Perhaps the most interesting contrasts at Hascombe Court are provided by the changes of level from sweeping lawns and herbaceous borders to sloping hollows and woodland walks, and also by the informality of much of the garden set against the yew hedges, terraces and seats which provide the architectural bones of the layout. Below the upper terrace on the south front, a second terrace linked by flights of stone steps at each end has as its focal point a recessed, semi-circular lily pool and

fountain. Enclosed on three sides by walls, the terrace has generous flower borders and topiary, while steps lead down past a paved lavender walk to a delightful Japanese rock garden. The upper terrace extends between yew and lavender beds to a formal garden centred on a fine lead fountain group designed by Lady Hilton Young, with beds filled with tulips in the spring, followed later in the season by delphiniums, lupins and penstemons. Beyond the West Terrace a spacious lawn extends to the woodland boundary, where a circular lily pool enclosed by yew hedges terminates the view. An idyllic spring walk runs between borders of azaleas, lilies and Japanese maples to a spectacular Bamboo Stairway forming a tunnel.

At the edges of the winding paths are hybrid rhododendrons, including 'Pink Pearl' and 'Britannia', the last producing striking crimson flowers. On the lower slopes, *Rhododendron arboreum, R. thomsonii* and the early-flowering *R. praecox* flourish, and in the spring the ground beneath is carpeted with narcissi and many different kinds of flowering bulbs.

From the lower part of the garden, steps lead up to Brenda's Walk, which skirts the valley and is planted with laburnums and berberis, with orange and yellow lilies and with delphiniums. A glade leads through a wild garden with flowering crabs and cherries to a spectacular, double herbaceous border terminated at the far end by an open-fronted summerhouse.

It is one of the characteristics of Hascombe Court that the gardens not only provide a delightful setting for the house, but relate successfully to the wonderful Surrey countryside that surrounds the property.

Open from April to July, on selected days.

Terraces spread down from the house to the Japanese Rock Garden

Waterlilies on the village pond

CHIDDINGFOLD
Surrey

6 MILES (9.5 KM) SOUTH OF GODALMING

Sunday, 13 November 1825
'We came through Chiddingfold, a very pretty place. There is a very pretty and extensive green opposite the church, and we were at the proper time of day to perceive that the modern system of education had by no means overlooked this little village. We saw the schools marching towards the church in military order.'
William Cobbett, *Rural Rides* (1830)

Lying in a fold or 'forest clearing' of undulating countryside, Chiddingfold boasts all the ingredients of perfection. At one corner of its large, triangular green cluster the church, an ancient inn, a 17th-century working forge, a pond and some Georgian houses. In the 13th century this was the main centre of the forest glass industry. Introduced by the Normans and using local charcoal and sand, it supplied stained glass far and wide until the industry declined in the 17th century with competition from the Midlands and the Forest of Dean. Little glass remains here, but the church has one lancet window made up of pieces found on old glasswork sites. The churchyard, entered through a lych-gate that still has its timber coffin rest, is adrift with wild crocuses in spring. Many of the beautiful buildings around the green date from the heyday of the glass industry, notably the timber-framed, 14th-century Crown Inn, one of the oldest in England. Its exposed external beams were originally tile-hung. Other houses and cottages are brick and tile-hung. At one time cattle would have grazed on the green and watered in the pond, and stray livestock would have been impounded within the walls of the village pound that stand in the garden of Pound Cottage, just off the green.

CLANDON PARK
Surrey

WEST CLANDON, 3 MILES (5 KM) EAST OF GUILDFORD

*P*erhaps it is unusual for the tour of a house to begin with its climax, but this is certainly the case at Clandon Park. Its magnificent two-storeyed Marble Hall has a superb plaster ceiling from which the legs of the figures hang down over the classical entablature. The house was built by the Venetian architect, Giacomo Leoni, in about 1733 for the 2nd Lord Onslow, and the series of rooms on show are beautifully proportioned and splendidly furnished.

When the National Trust acquired Clandon Park it was empty and the contents we see today are the result of a generous bequest by Mrs David Gubbay, of Little Trent Park in Hertfordshire. Mrs Gubbay's legacy included the wonderful collection of porcelain which is on display all around the house, the highlights of which include the extraordinarily delicate Commedia dell' Arte figures and a unique and colourful assortment of 17th- and 18th-century Chinese birds. The furniture includes some outstanding examples of marquetry work and there is some fine needlework on display.

The old kitchen, with its fascinating array of old pots, pans and utensils, and the Museum of the Queen's Royal Surrey Regiment are in the cellar.

In the gardens, which extend to about seven acres (2.8ha), is the delightful Maori House, brought from New Zealand in 1892.

Open from April to October, most afternoons. Tel: 01483 222482.

Clandon's rather austere exterior hides a wonderful marble hall and other treasures

A WALK AT
FRIMLEY GREEN

*F*rimley Green is 3½miles (5km) south of Camberley on the A321. The walk starts from Frimley Lodge Park, next to the church. For the parking area, drive into the park, bear right and follow the signs 'Canal South & Trim Trail'; the parking area is by the miniature railway.

From Frimley Lodge Park the walk goes along the canal then through woodland of pine and silver birch on sandy paths. Look out for grey squirrels, and woodland birds can be seen among the pine trees throughout the year; fungi, such as the colourful but poisonous fly agaric, abound in autumn. There are pike in the canal, where moorhens can usually be seen.

The miniature railway at Frimley Lodge Park

The walk is about 1½ miles (2.4km) long, and level, easy walking, with one short flight of fairly steep wooden steps. Seats along the canal offer places to pause, and the nearby King's Head pub has a garden and play area for children.

🐑🐑🐑🐑

DIRECTIONS

From the car park walk a few yards up the track to the canal. Turn right onto the towpath and continue for about ¾ mile (1.2km) to the road bridge. Go up the steps and turn left across the bridge. Opposite Potters pub, turn left along a track and bear right along the

signposted bridleway. Almost immediately bear left off the main path along a narrow footpath.

Continue through the pine woods at the back of a school, keeping to the left wherever there is a choice. On reaching the marked bridleway turn left and keep left at the next signpost. Remain on this path for about ¾ mile and eventually emerge on to Windmill Lane.

Continue ahead to the road, turn left and after a few yards cross the narrow bridge over the canal (with care – there is no pavement). A few yards ahead is the King's Head pub. Take the path to the left, immediately after the bridge, leading back down to the canal towpath. Turn right and return along the canal to the car park.

Frimley Lodge Park
Covering nearly 70 acres (28ha) of meadowland and mature woodland, Frimley Lodge Park includes formal

The Basingstoke Canal, built in the late 18th century to link Basingstoke and London

play areas, picnic sites with barbecue facilities, a trim trail, a miniature railway (which operates on selected Sunday afternoons), a pitch and putt course and a pavilion with a cafeteria.

The Canal
Built between 1789 and 1794, the Basingstoke Canal was once busy with barges carrying timber for ship- and house-building, grain, malt and other produce from north Hampshire to London, returning with cargoes of coal and manufactured goods. It was formally re-opened in 1991 by HRH The Duke of Kent after a long programme of restoration begun in 1974.

The canal is stocked with fish, and day fishing tickets can be purchased at all local tackle shops. They must be obtained in advance.

POLESDEN LACEY
Surrey

3 MILES (5 KM) NORTH-WEST OF DORKING

The previous house on this site was owned by the playwright Richard Brinsley Sheridan, but his only remaining legacy here is the long terraced walk, the most impressive feature of the garden. Two years after his death the property was sold to Joseph Bonsor, who commissioned the large, but pleasantly unpretentious house we see today.

Polesden Lacey really came into its own during the Edwardian era, when the estate belonged to the Hon Ronald Greville and his wife. Until the outbreak of World War II the house was alive with high society gatherings, presided over by the vivacious Mrs Greville. The daughter of the Right

Hon William McEwan, one-time Member of Parliament and founder of the McEwan brewery, she was a charming but determined lady with high social ambitions. Through her husband's connections she found her way into the Marlborough House circle of Edward VII, and after her husband died in 1908 she capitalised on those introductions until she was a much sought-after hostess, entertaining the King and his friends on a lavish scale at Polesden Lacey. The Duke and Duchess of York (later George VI and Queen Elizabeth), spent part of their honeymoon here. The visitors' books, menus, photographs and newspaper cuttings which survive here are,

The rooms are beautifully furnished with family treasures, below, while right, terraced lawns sweep away from the house

perhaps, the most telling reminders of the high life they all enjoyed.

'Ronnie' Greville's enormous strength of character still permeates Polesden Lacey to this day, and her fine collections of paintings, tapestries, porcelain and other works of art furnish the house in handsome style. On her death in 1942 she bequeathed the house to the National Trust as a memorial to her father. She herself is buried in the grounds.

The interior of the house consists of a series of fascinating rooms ranged around a central courtyard; the entrance hall, two storeys high, is both welcoming and impressive. The dining room, scene of Mrs Greville's sumptuous dinner parties, has some beautiful silver and porcelain, and the drawing room has carved and gilt panelling that may have come from an Italian palace. Most of the art collection is displayed in the corridor around the courtyard, and includes the work of Italian and Dutch artists.

In keeping both with its literary origins and the era of great social gatherings, Polesden Lacey now stages an open-air theatre season during the summer.

Open most afternoons from April to October; weekends only during March and November. Tel: 01372 458203 or 452048.

STREET HOUSE
Surrey

THURSLEY, 5 MILES (8 KM) SOUTH-WEST OF GODALMING

The deep Surrey countryside boasts many gardens both large and small, but few can match the important historical associations and charm of Street House, at Thursley, between Milford and Hindhead. In the fine Regency house the great architect Sir Edwin Lutyens spent his early and most formative years, and it was while he was designing Crooksbury, his first commission, in this house that he met Gertrude Jekyll, who was to have such a lasting influence both on him and on the design of the great ensemble of Edwardian country house and garden epitomised by their unique partnership.

The attractive 1827 house stands behind a row of imposing lime trees underplanted with lady's mantle, and as you turn the corner of the building to enter the 1¹/₂ acre (0.5ha) garden, a glance behind reveals a view of the village church framed by three sycamore trees. It soon becomes apparent that there are three separate gardens at Street House. At the back, a curved island bed in the centre of a spacious lawn spills over with purple delphiniums, white foxgloves and lupins, underplanted with *Stachys lanata* and *Alchemilla mollis*.

Below this, on the mezzanine level, is a circular astrological mandala, incorporating a small round pond. It was built by the present owner, Mrs B M Francis, in local ironstone and Bargate stone unearthed from the garden. Near by, in the Lower Garden, in a secluded corner edged by artemisias and *Lonicera nitida* 'Baggesen's Gold', is a wooden seat designed by Lutyens, and a short flight of stone steps brings you past a spiky verbascum to the main lawn at the side of the house. The walled garden is full of unusual and interesting plants, trees and shrubs, including *Rubus x tridel*, the thornless shrub with peeling bark which produces white, rose-like flowers in early summer, and a great acacia, *Robinia pseudoacacia*.

Street House boasts a magnificent *Cornus kousa*, a Japanese snowball tree, some rare old-fashioned roses including *Rosa mundi*, and 'Cardinal Richelieu', 'Blue Diamond' rhododendrons and camellias. From the gardens there is also a wonderful view towards the Devil's Punch Bowl, one of Surrey's most famous beauty spots.

Open on selected days during the summer.

Above, signs in the stonework of the astrological mandala

Left, a charmingly overgrown path

Far left, a view across the garden to the village church

*Still a family home, Arundel
reflects the changes of nearly
a thousand years*

ARUNDEL CASTLE
West Sussex

ARUNDEL, 12 MILES (19 KM) EAST OF CHICHESTER

The charming palace-castle which sprawls among the trees in this attractive West Sussex town has so many battlemented towers and chimneys that it has an almost fairy-tale appearance. There has been a castle at Arundel for some 900 years, ever since a castle mound was raised in about 1088. Around 100 years later, a circular shell keep was built on the mound and at the same time, or perhaps a little later, walls, a chapel and a garden were added by Henry II. It is possible that this was the first royal garden in England.

Most of the castle, however, is more recent, and owes much to the work of the 11th Duke of Norfolk, who, in 1787, began to renovate and reconstruct Arundel so that it could become his main home outside London. Subsequent Dukes have continued this work, and today there are many splendid rooms packed with treasures on view to the public. The collection of paintings is especially fine, containing works by such artists as Van Dyck, Lely, Reynolds, Lawrence and Gainsborough.

In the chapel, marble columns soar upwards to gothic arches and an intriguing striped ceiling, and many of the state rooms contain exquisite furnishings.

Open from April to October, daily except Sunday. Tel: 01903 883136.

BODIAM CASTLE
East Sussex

12 MILES (19 KM) NORTH OF HASTINGS

With its battlemented walls and towers reflected in a moat dotted with water-lilies, Bodiam is one of the most picturesque castles in Britain. But beauty was hardly the prime objective of Bodiam's builder when he constructed his castle and dug his moat – this was a fortress designed to repel invaders and to provide a haven of safety for those lucky enough to be secure within its walls.

Bodiam was built by Sir Edward Dalyngrygge between 1385 and 1388. Richard II had granted him a licence to fortify his manor house after the nearby port of Rye had been attacked by the French. Interpreting the licence somewhat more liberally than had been intended, Dalyngrygge promptly abandoned his old manor house and set about building Bodiam Castle.

The castle is rectangular, with a round tower at each corner and a square tower midway along each wall; two of these square towers form gateways. Bodiam is totally surrounded by the wide moat, across which a series of bridges originally gave access to the castle, some at right angles to each other to prevent storming. These elaborate defences against attack were never seriously tested – Bodiam was involved in a skirmish in 1484, but during the Civil War it was surrendered without a shot being fired.

Open all year, except Mondays between November and March, and Christmas. Tel: 01580 830436.

Bodiam Castle remains relatively intact today, proof of its peaceful past

BURPHAM
West Sussex

3 MILES (5 KM) NORTH-EAST OF ARUNDEL

This is a lovely place, at the end of a lane that winds north from the A27, leads round the village, then goes no further. The Saxons built defensive earthworks here to try and keep the marauding Danes at bay and today they make a good viewpoint: north over the village to the South Downs; south to Arundel's medieval-looking castle (completed in fact in 1903); and west across a languorous loop of the River Arun and its watermeadows to a stretch of the Wey and Arun Canal, built as a short-cut in the 19th century. Flint and brick cottages, some with thatched roofs, some tiled, nestle in the trees round the squat, flint church. St Mary's is mostly 12th- and 13th-century and has a good Norman interior, white and spacious, with exuberant carving on the pillars. It incorporates some Roman tiles and there are the remains of a Roman pavement near the north transept. Near the church is the George and Dragon, a pub with a long history of smuggling connections. From the grassy open space a footpath follows steps down to the riverbank. On the village's south-eastern outskirts, at Lea Farm on Wepham Down, there was a leper colony in the Middle Ages, from which a track south known as Lepers' Way took its name.

The village as seen from the earthworks

BURWASH
East Sussex

5 MILES (8 KM) EAST OF HEATHFIELD

Old shops and cottages form an almost unbroken line in the high street

The wealth of a bygone era is immediately recognisable in the number of prestigious old houses in Burwash, a village of exceptional beauty and harmony spread along a ridge of the Weald between the Rivers Dudwell and Rother. The soil of the Weald has always been rich in iron, and between the 15th and the 17th centuries foundries by the dozen were smelting the ore, supplying the arms and armour for the country's conquering heroes. Burwash was one of the main centres of this Wealden iron industry and some of its most striking buildings are old ironmasters' houses. The houses and cottages of the village, timber-framed, stuccoed, mellow brick and tile-hung, are mainly in one long, wide street lined with pollarded limes. One of the best is Rampyndene, a large brick and tile-hung house with majestically tall chimneys, built in 1699 by a timber merchant. Timber merchants, of course, prospered from the iron industry too, for it depended on the oaks of the local forests – extensive at that time – for the charcoal needed for smelting. The church, which has an early Norman tower, has some early iron tomb slabs. Bateman's is a fine stone-built Jacobean house just south of the village, built in 1634 by a local ironmaster. From 1902 to 1936 it was the home of Rudyard Kipling.

Bateman's at Burwash
Rudyard Kipling and his wife bought Bateman's in 1902 and stayed there until they died, he in 1936, she in 1939. The 300 acre (122ha) estate was laid out by Mrs Kipling. Works he wrote while living here include *Puck of Pook's Hill* and the poem 'If'. Bateman's is now in the hands of the National Trust and visitors can see Kipling's rooms and study as they were in his lifetime. His 1928 Rolls Royce is on show in its garage.

Delphiniums of deepest blue

DENMANS
West Sussex

FONTWELL, 4½ MILES (7 KM) EAST OF CHICHESTER

Nestling below the South Downs is the beautiful 3½ acre (1.5ha) garden of Denmans. Like all really distinguished gardens, it is continually changing and repays regular visits by both plant lovers and those interested in garden design, because, since 1985, it has been managed by the landscape designer and author, John Brookes. Mrs Joyce Robinson, the present owner, and her husband, bought the estate in 1946, and with the exception of a great cedar of Lebanon, planted in the early 19th century, and some old pears, all the trees that give the garden its form today have been introduced by Mrs Robinson.

At the end of the gravel path leading from the car park, the planting is striking and individual. A great clump of euphorbias grows outside

Planting of blue and silver gives way to white and gold

the tea shop, while in a nearby bed viburnums, weigela and laurel flourish, fringed by achilleas, purple sage and lady's mantle. Four foliage beds have also been planted, rather like a colour-coding for the main garden. In the first bed the theme is silver and white, so *Lamium* 'Molten Silver', hebes, *Stachys lanata* and verbascums predominate. The red bed shows *Berberis thunbergii,* a dark-leaved bergenia and an elder, while the two remaining beds are devoted to gold plants and to a collection of grasses.

The conservatory houses tender plants, with clematis 'Vyvyan Pennell' showing mauve flowers in spring, contrasting with two beautiful abutilons, one peach-coloured and the other red. Over the entrance to the nearby walled garden, *Clematis montana* 'Rubrum' cascades, and the sinuous gravel path and the dense planting soon transports you into another world, one dominated by a tall *Eucalyptus gunnii* underplanted with honeysuckle, philadelphus, purple lilac and a robust yellow peony.

The main garden slopes south, with a large lawn broken up by a dry gravel 'stream' that runs down to a pond. At the top is a splendid group of trees which includes a cherry and a whitebeam. Stone bridges cross the 'stream', and bamboo and willow grow alongside viburnums, phormiums and the Mexican orange blossom. Instead of pebbles, the pond is filled with water, and waterlilies punctuate its surface. Among the trees are a *Cupressus arizonica*, a great dawn redwood, a ginkgo and a tulip tree, as well as two red oaks shading a small orchard. Here, sitting on a seat in a sunny corner, is an ideal place to admire the beauty and the design of this most charming and diverse of gardens.

Open daily, from March to December. Tel: 01243 542808.

A small statue sits patiently beside the lily pond

Herstmonceux, one of the most striking 15th-century castles in Britain

HERSTMONCEUX CASTLE
East Sussex

8 MILES (13 KM) NORTH OF EASTBOURNE

Many people will associate the fine brick palace at Herstmonceux with the Royal Observatory, which moved here from Greenwich in 1948. In 1989 the Royal Observatory moved yet again, leaving Herstmonceux to adjust to its new existence as a conference centre. It was one of the first castles in England to be built of brick, and the effect is stunning. Its clusters of elegant chimneys and the many towers, all in a pleasing shade of rich red, are reflected in the wide moat that surrounds it, rendering it one of the most attractive castles built in the Middle Ages.

Sir Roger Fiennes was granted a licence to build Herstmonceux in 1441.

The fact that the castle was built in a lake afforded some protection, and the impressive gatehouse presented a formidable array of murder holes and arrow slits with which to greet hostile visitors.

Once the castle had passed from the Fiennes family, it had a sad history of careless owners. In the 17th century, one owner shamelessly ripped the interior of the castle out in order to provide himself with the raw materials to build another house, and a great deal of work has been necessary to restore it to its former grandeur.

The castle is not open to the public, but the grounds are open at certain times of year. Tel: 01323 833913.

※

STANDEN
West Sussex

1½ MILES (2 KM) SOUTH OF EAST GRINSTEAD

※

Standen is a charming tribute to the Arts and Crafts movement of the 19th century

*T*his delightful house was built between 1891 and 1894 by Philip Webb for the Beale family and is a showpiece of the 19th-century Arts and Crafts movement. Webb, along with William Morris, was a leading light in the movement, whose main principles concerned the promotion of craftsmanship as opposed to the mass-production of the Victorian age. Generally the architect would specify not only the building design but also the interior fittings and furniture, and Standen has some beautifully preserved William Morris wallpapers and fabrics. His designs here include the famous Sunflower, Peacock, Trellis and Larkspur motifs, among others.

The furniture was also custom made and includes contemporary brass beds from Heal's, furniture from the Morris company and ceramics by William de Morgan. Webb himself designed some of the furniture, as well as such details as the fire grates, the electric light fittings and the finger-plates for the doors.

Standen is a rambling house which looks for all the world as if it had developed over many centuries, rather than having been completed in a relatively short space of time, and this is due to Webb's use of the vernacular style and traditional building materials.

Open most afternoons from April to October and weekends in March. Tel: 01342 323029.

Flint walls and period houses line the street that has changed little in layout since the 16th century

FULKING
West Sussex

7 MILES (11 KM) NORTH-WEST OF BRIGHTON

HE SENDETH SPRINGS INTO THE VALLEYS WHICH RUN AMONG THE HILLS OH THAT MEN WOULD PRAISE THE LORD FOR HIS GOODNESS!

(Inscription on the tiles of the pump-house)

The story that Fulking has to tell has much to do with sheep, the sheep that used to graze the South Downs in numbers that few of us today will remember. A stream flows down to the road from the steep escarpment behind the village and in late spring all the local shepherds would dam it up, closing the road temporarily, in order to wash their sheep before the shearing gangs set to work. At the end of the day, the shepherds and their dogs would relax in the Shepherd and Dog Inn. The springs that feed the stream used to be the village's only water supply and in Victorian times a pump-house was built beside the road to provide water, free and for ever, for the villagers of Fulking. This was used until the 1950s when mains water was brought here. The village has its pub and it has that other bastion, the shop, albeit struggling for survival like others, but it is unusual in never having had a church. Among its houses are some small architectural gems, several mentioned in the *Domesday Book,* and several dating from the 15th and 16th centuries. With easy walks up on to the Downs on the old sheep paths, this is a delightful place in which to pause.

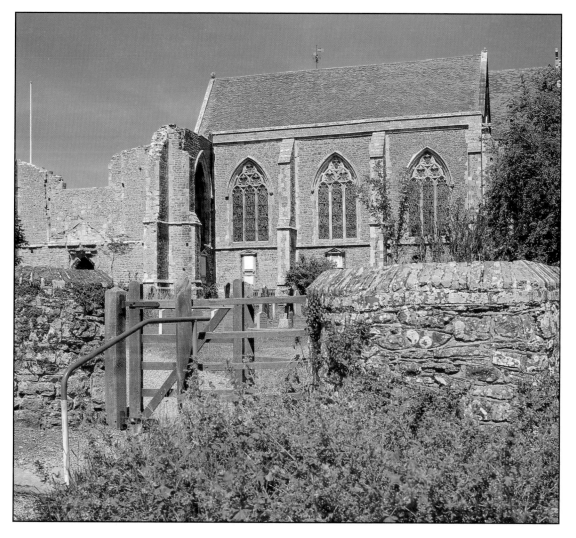

St Thomas's Church, planned
on a vast scale but never
completed

WINCHELSEA
East Sussex

10 MILES (16 KM) EAST OF HASTINGS

'Tew' Winchelsea stands on a hill, well above the sea that in the 13th century drowned the original Winchelsea, the town that had joined the confederation of Cinque Ports in 1191. The new town was built by Edward I to replace the old, as a defensive port and centre for the wine trade with France. But the sea is a law unto itself and before long it receded, leaving Winchelsea stuck on the marshes, a mile inland. Its harbour silted up and trading collapsed, the French kept raiding, the Black Death swept through and Winchelsea went into decline. Similar fates befell other places but what is so individual is its layout. Within defensive walls

that have survived in part to this day, Edward I used a grid pattern for the streets and although his buildings have mostly gone, the plan remains. Three of the 14th-century town gates guard the entrances, and the 14th-century chancel of the Church of St Thomas, all that was ever finished, survives, complete with a contemporary wall-painting and monuments. Medieval wine vaults can be seen beneath some of the inns, and the court house, now a museum, is a reminder of the days of prosperity – but mostly it is red-roofed houses, tile-hung and white-painted, that line the chequerboard streets of this peaceful and beautiful village.

Winchelsea and Rye
An historic patina covers their buildings more deeply than any others, in England at least. Indeed, I know of no place save for Paris, where memories seem so thick on every stone.
Ford Madox Ford, *Return to Yesterday* (1932)

GREAT DIXTER
East Sussex

NORTHIAM, 7 MILES (11 KM) NORTH-WEST OF RYE

*T*he name of Great Dixter will be familiar to all who read Christopher Lloyd's regular contributions on gardening in *Country Life*, but the lively inventiveness of his horticultural style none the less comes as a surprise however often you visit the garden. The medieval manor was bought by Nathaniel Lloyd in 1910, and Sir Edwin Lutyens was commissioned to design the gardens, and the steps and terraces that still provide the framework of the layout are distinctly his. The sunken garden, the topiary and the yew and box hedging were the responsibility of the owner, while his wife, Daisy, created the wild moat garden and continued to help develop the garden in conjunction with her son, Christopher, after her husband's death.

The gardens at Dixter totally surround the 15th-century manor house, and the lane from Northiam brings you to the north side, a flagstone path leading straight through a lovely meadow area to the medieval porch. In summer yellow and orange lilies grow in pots to brighten the timber-framed façade, while ferns flourish beneath the windows, and the lawn supports a Chilean bamboo and an old common pear. Near by, on this north side, is the colourful sunken garden with an octagonal pool

Left, the timber-framed manor house provides an attractive focus for this country garden

Above, a flash of kniphofia lends colour to the moat

surrounded by drystone walls, the enclosure framed by barn walls and a yew hedge. Ferns and Kenilworth ivy grow out of crevices in the paving, and geraniums and lavender support the rich border-planting of campanulas, astrantias, *Eryngium giganteum*, variegated euonymus, day lilies and lychnis.

In the walled garden, spare a glance for the *Clematis x jouiniana* 'Praecox', and for the blue thistles, euphorbias and mallows, before leaving via a flight of steps characteristic of Lutyens' style. Continue past a bed of hydrangeas, rodgersias and geraniums to the topiary lawn, inhabited by great birds and abstract shapes in clipped yew. The old moat is seeded with grasses and is bright in spring with moon daisies, knapweed and clover, while a splendid magnolia makes a dramatic seasonal show.

The Long Border is strong in colour contrasts, with golden elder and Mount Etna broom set against white hydrangeas, variegated golden hostas and mahonia. Sea hollies make a regular appearance, while the blue of *Campanula lactiflora*, euonymus 'Silver Queen' and pink diascias contribute to a rich display. The golden shower of *Ulmus* 'Dicksonii' attracts the eye in the middle of the border with silver-grey willows underplanted with blue veronica and purple everlasting peas.

Open from April to October, afternoons except Monday, and on other selected days. Tel: 01797 252878.

Right, the sturdy yew hedges which form the enclosures in this lovely garden were laid out by Nathaniel Lloyd to give protection to more tender plants

Below, a path of rough-cut flagstones leads through the topiary

BLUEBELL RAILWAY
East Sussex

SHEFFIELD PARK, 15 MILES (24 KM) NORTH-EAST OF BRIGHTON

*I*t is little wonder that the Bluebell Railway is probably the best-known preserved railway in Britain. Re-opened in 1960, it is the oldest of the former British Railways lines to be saved by preservationists – and one of its engines, *Stepney*, was used as the basis of an engine character by the Reverend W Awdry in his perennially popular children's books. Even those who have not heard of the Bluebell may recognise its southern terminus, since it takes its name from the nearby National Trust garden of Sheffield Park.

It is worth spending some time at Sheffield Park, admiring the superbly overhauled and repainted locomotives turned out by the well-equipped workshops, and looking at the small museum and model railway on the platform opposite the entrance. The location of the signal box on the platform allows visitors to appreciate the burnished brass instruments and steel levers at closer quarters than most preserved railways.

Having been first in the field, the Bluebell was at a great advantage when it came to buying both locomotives and carriages from British Rail.

Crew taking a breather at Horsted Keynes

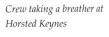

Steam traction still had eight years to run on Britain's national railways so there were over 10,000 locomotives and hundreds of different classes from which to choose. No railway can rival the Bluebell for the variety and antiquity of its coaches – many date from before World War I and few were built after the second. To sit in a beautifully upholstered compartment, surrounded by polished wood, ornate brass fittings and prints of rail destinations is one of the particular pleasures of a journey on the line.

Another hallmark of the Bluebell is attention to detail when it comes to authenticity, for few railways have been as particular in the way stations or rolling stock have been restored. The correct colours are scrupulously applied, and a journey from Sheffield Park takes passengers on something of a trip through time: this station has been renovated in the style of the London Brighton & South Coast Railway which built the line, opening in 1882; Horsted Keynes exemplifies a Southern Railway country junction of the 1930s; and the northern terminus at Kingscote, re-opened in 1994 as part of the drive to rejoin British Rail at East Grinstead, is being renovated in the style of the 1950s. The journey also takes passengers from the eastern hemisphere to the west, crossing the line of the Greenwich

South Eastern & Chatham Railway P class 0-6-0T No 323, Bluebell, *one of the line's oldest – and smallest – locomotives*

Workmanlike No 847 waiting at Sheffield Park for another passenger load

Meridian as it leaves Sheffield Park.

The train accelerates past the elegant starting signal at Sheffield Park so that the locomotive can get to grips with the steep 2-mile (3km) climb up Freshfield Bank. The woods that follow give the railway its name, for in May they are a mass of bluebells, almost irridescent in dappled spring sunshine. It is hard to believe that this idyllic countryside was the centre of Britain's iron industry during the Middle Ages, but woods like those beside the line were the source of the charcoal upon which the industry depended.

A final climb through a cutting brings the train into the imposing four-platform station at Horsted Keynes. The size of the station – even equipped with a subway – is astonishing for so remote a location, but this was once the junction for a line to Haywards Heath that was still in use when the Bluebell began operations. The route of the line, which closed in 1963, can be seen going off behind the signal box on the left on the approach to the station. Apart from the country park, ideal for picnics or for children to let off steam, Horsted Keynes has the Bluebell's carriage and wagon works and sheds, where the varied skills needed to maintain the stock are practised. It is also worth allowing time for a drink in the delightfully restored bar on the middle platform, which must have consoled many a weary traveller waiting for a connection.

Out of Horsted Keynes, another climb faces northbound trains as they approach Sharpthorne Tunnel, at 780yds (714m) the longest tunnel on any preserved railway. The pictures of Kingscote station before a team began work following its purchase in 1985 are a good indication of what dedicated volunteers can achieve. An entire platform had to be replaced, and the filled-in subway cleared out – quite apart from the eradication of both wet and dry rot in the station building.

Visitors to the Bluebell from the London area can take advantage of a vintage bus service that runs non-stop from East Grinstead station to Kingscote, a ten-minute journey, every day that the railway operates and to coincide with the trains. Only visitors arriving at Kingscote by this bus are entitled to buy a ticket here, because of parking restrictions around the station. In a few years it should be possible to reach the Bluebell Railway by a simple cross-platform change at East Grinstead.

Train service: daily over Easter week and from May to September, then weekends to December and Sundays from January to March. Tel: 01825 722370.

Frequent routine checks are carried out when the trains are operating

BRIGHTON
East Sussex

48 MILES (77 KM) SOUTH OF LONDON

*I*n 1753 a certain Dr Richard Russell of Lewes moved to an obscure fishing village named Brighthelmstone on the south coast. A skilful publicist, he successfully trumpeted the medical virtues of sea air, sea bathing and even drinking sea water, judiciously mixed with milk. He also promoted a mineral spring called St Ann's Well in nearby Hove. From these bracing beginnings developed the splendidly self-indulgent acknowledged queen of British seaside resorts, with its elegant Regency terraces, squares and crescents, its grand Victorian churches, its piers and promenade and aquarium, its smart shops, restaurants and racecourse, its ice-cream parlours and whelk stalls and every variety of seaside amusement from the raffish to the exquisite. The most important single visitor in the early days was the Prince Regent, afterwards George IV. He first

Uncrowned Queen

Ever since it became fashionable, Brighton has attracted lovers. The precedent was set by the future George IV himself, who spent an idyllic summer honeymoon here with his new and entirely illegal bride, Mrs Fitzherbert. The charming Maria Anne Fitzherbert was twice widowed, and possessed of a modest fortune and an immodestly enticing figure when the Prince went through a secret marriage with her in London in 1785, in flagrant breach of the Royal Marriages Act. She took a house in Brighton, which was later rumoured to be connected to the Royal Pavilion by a secret passage, but the relationship went through many ups and downs. The Prince could not acknowledge her without losing the throne, and he finally brusquely broke off with her in 1811. She died in 1837 and lies buried near the altar of the Roman Catholic church of St John the Baptist in Kemp Town

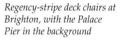

Regency-stripe deck chairs at Brighton, with the Palace Pier in the background

came here in 1783, later took a house and eventually employed the architect John Nash to build him a stately pleasure-dome, the Royal Pavilion, a wonderful oriental fantasy with dazzling Chinese-style interiors, imitation bamoo everywhere and a kitchen staffed by serried ranks of gleaming copper pans. Brighton's fashionable reputation was made, and the town expanded rapidly – eastwards to Kemp Town and to the west until it bumped into Hove. The oldest part of the town is the area called the Lanes, a warren of narrow alleys, smart boutiques and antique shops. The grandly domed Palace Pier, completed in 1901, replaced the earlier Chain Pier, which had been swept away in a ferocious storm. The West Pier of 1886 is now sadly derelict.

Among the churches, the parish church of Brighton is St Peter's, designed by Sir Charles Barry in the 1820s. The huge brick barn of St Bartholomew's in Ann Street – locally nicknamed 'Noah's Ark' – has a striking Art Nouveau Byzantine-style interior. Hove has its own sumptuous Regency squares and terraces, and an impressive Victorian legacy in the form of a working steam museum of vast hissing machines in a restored pumping station. Meanwhile the old Volk's Electric Railway rattles along the eastern part of the sea front to the enormous marina. The Hotel Metropole is the finishing point of the famous London to Brighton Veteran Car Run, an annual commemoration of the raising of the speed limit, in 1896, from 4mph to 12mph.

A concert in the charming bandstand, with the pier in the distance

EASTBOURNE
East Sussex

19 MILES (31 KM) EAST OF BRIGHTON

Sheltered by the South Downs and the bulk of Beachy Head, Eastbourne basks in an exceptionally high sunshine count and a reputation for restrained middle-class charm which dates back to the mid-19th century, when it first blossomed as a seaside resort. The original village is a mile inland from the sea front, clustered round the medieval church of St Mary, and the 'bourne' or stream from which the town takes its name still runs to the sea concealed beneath Bourne Street.

and Devonshire Place, where the Duke is commemorated by a fine statue. The handsome brick church of St Saviour was built in the 1860s, and development continued to create 'the Empress of Watering Places', with grand hotels, comfortable villas, smart shops and attractive parks. The great Eugenius Birch designed the pier. At the edge of the shingle beach the promenade runs on three levels, with municipal flower gardens along the top. Cannons are ready to repel invaders on The

God gives all men all earth to love,

But, since man's heart is small, Ordains for each one spot shall prove

Beloved over all.

Each to his choice, and I rejoice

The lot has fallen to me

In a fair ground – in a fair ground

Yea, Sussex by the sea!

Rudyard Kipling, *Sussex* (1902)

The 18th-century manor house is now the Towner Art Gallery, where a rewarding array of British art of the 19th and 20th centuries includes a major collection of work by the Eastbourne artist and designer Eric Ravilious. After centuries of inconspicuous existence, Eastbourne was developed as a resort in the 1850s, principally by the seventh Duke of Devonshire, who owned much of it. The imposing Grand Parade was laid out along the front, and terraces of houses went up in Cavendish Place

Redoubt, a fortress built early in the 19th century which now houses an engagingly grotto-like aquarium and a military museum. Lifeboats from the earliest days of the service to the present are on view in the country's first lifeboat museum, opened here in 1937. Up on the sheer cliff of Beachy Head (which holds such an attraction for suicides that the Samaritans have a special sign there), a new visitor centre is being built to focus attention on the beauty of the downland with its rare orchids and butterflies and its superb views over the Channel.

The municipal flower beds bloom brightly along the front at Eastbourne

PEVENSEY
East Sussex

4 MILES (6 KM) NORTH-EAST OF EASTBOURNE

The walls of Pevensey Castle, with the church of St Nicolas in the background

Helping Hands

Local criminals were tried in the Court House at Pevensey and there was an old tradition that a freeman of Pevensey, if condemned to death, had the right to die by drowning rather than hanging. The condemned man's hands and feet were bound and he was then thrown into the harbour. A pile of stones was kept handy to pelt him with if he was slow to succumb.

Pevensey has been fortified against invaders and marauders ever since Roman times, when the powerful stronghold of *Anderida* was constructed in the 3rd century AD as one of the forts of the Saxon Shore. After the Romans had gone, it was besieged by the Saxon warlord Aelle and his son Cissa, who took it and slaughtered everyone inside – men, women and children. The massive Roman walls are still standing up to 20ft (7m) high in places, incorporated into Pevensey Castle (English Heritage), which was built soon after the Norman Conquest by Count Robert of Mortain, half-brother of William the Conqueror. It was somewhere near this spot that William

had landed with his invasion force in 1066, among sea-flooded marshes studded with small islands, or 'eyes', of which Pevensey was one. It had its own harbour until the sea receded. In 1940 the castle resumed its ancient duties when it was re-armed with a gun emplacement as part of the coastal defences against a possible German invasion – a refortification which was fortunately never tested. Close to the fortress, for protection, is the village with its tough-looking church, dedicated to St Nicolas. Other old buildings of interest include the 15th-century Mint House, which is haunted by the ghost of a woman who was starved to death there, and the Court House, with a small museum.

HASTINGS
East Sussex

32 MILES (51 KM) EAST OF BRIGHTON

*I*t was to Hastings that William the Conqueror led his army after landing at Pevensey. The town was already an important port and continued to be, as a leading Cinque Port, until stormy seas blocked the harbour with shingle. Fishing boats are still drawn up on the shingle of the Stade at the eastern end of the front, and the old town lies inland from here, in a narrow valley between the high sandstone cliffs of the West Hill and the East Hill. There's a museum of local history in the old town hall, and the Shipwreck Heritage Centre displays material from important local wrecks. A cliff railway runs up West Hill, to the remains of the Norman castle and the '1066 Story' exhibition. The extensive St Clement's Caves, partly natural and partly man-made, are open to visitors as The Smugglers Adventure. Below, the 1820s church of St Mary with its Greek Revival-style portico is being restored. Modern Hastings developed to the west – on past the Victorian pier – as a healthful seaside resort from the later 18th century on, and neighbouring St Leonard's was elegantly laid out by James Burton and his son Decimus in the 1820s and 1830s.

Unique to Hastings are the 'deezes', tall huts for storing fishermen's nets

RYE HARBOUR

*R*ye Harbour, adjoining the mouth of the River Rother, is a large area of stabilised shingle with a wide range of breeding birds and winter visitors, together with an interesting shingle flora. Salt-marsh, pools and grazing marsh add to the variety. Birdwatching at Rye Harbour is excellent: terns, gulls and waders breed here and a wide variety of migrant and wintering species appears in varying numbers. In all, 260 species of bird have been recorded on the reserve.

The walk is about 4¾ miles (7.5 km), and easy walking on level ground. There is no shelter, so take windproof and waterproof clothing. The car park (free) lies roughly 1½ miles (2.4 km) south-east of Rye, on the minor road signposted to Rye Harbour from the town.

❀❀❀❀

DIRECTIONS

1 From the car park walk south-east along the metalled track signposted 'No through road' which runs parallel to the River Rother. Between the river and the track is a stretch of salt-marsh comprising mainly sea purslane. Viper's bugloss, mugwort, sea-beet and sea carrot grow beside the path, together with a few clumps of salsify. The fields to the right of the path should be scanned for yellow wagtails, buntings, larks and finches. Pause at the nature reserve

sign-board and view the small pool on the right either from the path or from the small hide. Black-headed gulls and redshanks are invariably present and migrant waders can be seen in spring and autumn.

2 Continue along the path until it reaches the seafront. Scan Rye Bay for birds. At low tide, the exposed sand of Rye Bay will have gulls and waders. At high tide during the winter months, look for divers, grebes and the occasional eider duck on the water.

Retrace your steps and follow the path which heads south-west, parallel to the sea. Do not stray from the path, and keep dogs on leads. (Ignore the public footpath sign to the right unless you wish to take a short cut leading past a hide at the northern end of the Ternery Pool and back to the car park.)

The shingle on either side of the track is covered with extensive patches of sea pea, sea kale, biting stonecrop, yellow horned poppy, birdsfoot trefoil, bittersweet and the shingle form of herb Robert. Look for small copper butterflies. Ringed plovers and wheatears are frequent nesters among the shingle, which is fenced off to the right of the path in order to protect them.

3 Make a detour from the main path to the Guy Crittall hide, which overlooks the

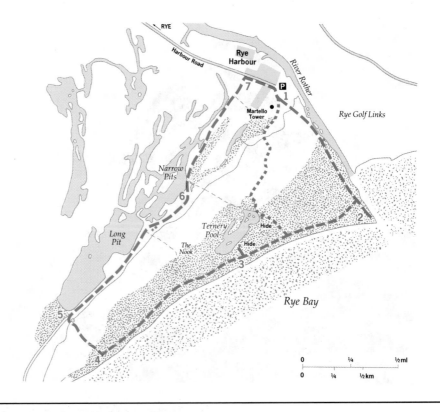

southern shore of the Ternery Pool. Shelducks, black-headed gulls, cormorants, coots, Canada geese, common terns, little grebes and oystercatchers are common in the summer months. A wide variety of waders can be seen during spring and autumn migration times. This is a good spot for unusual species: a rarely seen little egret spent several weeks here in the spring of 1990. Little terns can often be seen from the hide as they fly between fishing trips on the sea and their nests on the shingle.

4 At the reserve sign-board and map, turn right. The path is on shingle at first, but then follows a raised earth bank between two fields. Scan the fields for migrant birds and look for small skippers, gatekeepers and meadow brown butterflies, and plants including black horehound, burdock and pineapple mayweed beside the path.

5 At the footpath sign, turn right along a well-defined track and walk along the southern edge of the Long Pit. Look for gulls, grebes, cormorants and wildfowl on the water. Flocks of sparrows feed in the field to the right of the path and a few reed warblers sing from the overgrown drainage ditches. Look and listen for the occasional marsh frog. This large frog was introduced to Britain from the Continent as recently as 1935 and is now found in wetland areas around Romney Marsh, where it was first released.

6 Shortly after passing some farm buildings, the path runs around the margin of a reed-filled pool on the right of the track. Continue along the path, bearing left and keeping the edge of the Narrow Pits on your left. Look and listen for marsh frogs, reed warblers and reed buntings. Swallows and martins are common over the water in later summer and autumn. Turtle doves are common in the fields and often perch in pairs on the overhead wires. The path passes through areas of recently disturbed ground where colonising plants flourish. Look for mignonette, dark mullein and poppies.

7 After passing through a cement works, the path meets the road from Rye to Rye Harbour. Turn right and walk back to the car park.

❀

A WEALTH OF BREEDING BIRDS

Disturbance affects not only the shingle flowers but nesting birds as well – little terns, oystercatchers and ringed plovers lay their well-camouflaged eggs on the ground where they are vulnerable to trampling. Fortunately, sensitive areas are fenced off and visitors are asked to remain on the paths and keep dogs on leads. The Ternery Pool – a partly flooded gravel pit – is a focal point for nesting birds, which can be viewed from hides.

❀

MIGRANTS AND WINTER VISITORS

Outside the breeding season, birds of many different species pass through Rye Harbour, some remaining in the area for the winter. The pools and gravel pits act as focal points for a wide range of birds, especially waders, gulls and terns. Exactly which species are present varies not only from year to year but also from day to day and hour to hour, but avocets, spotted redshanks, black-tailed godwits, little stints, curlew sandpipers and green-shanks are all regular. Black terns, sometimes in small flocks, are seen in spring and autumn, and Mediterranean and little gulls are sometimes found by careful searching among the black-headed gulls.

❀

THE LITTLE TERN

This is our smallest breeding species of tern, with a length of only 9in (23cm). A summer visitor, the little tern arrives in April and departs for its wintering grounds on the African coast in September. Two or three eggs are laid in May on bare shingle or sand. Nests and incubating birds are vulnerable to attack by ground predators and disturbance by people. The nest colonies of terns – known as terneries – are now found in protected areas where wardens prevent disturbance. Rye Harbour Local Nature reserve holds one of the most important colonies in Britain.

Shingle Flora

At first glance, shingle appears to be so inhospitable that it is a wonder any plant can grow on it. However, a wide range of species thrives in this habitat, many of them never found anywhere else. These are specialist plants – species that can cope with the shifting, well-drained pebbles and the salt-laden environment. On the walk, look for yellow horned poppy, sea kale, sea pea, sea mayweed, sea rocket, haresfoot clover and biting stonecrop beside the waymarked paths. Where the shingle grades into salt-marsh and grazing meadow, slender hare's-ear and least lettuce are occasionally found. Disturbance and trampling are a major threat to shingle plants, and Rye Harbour is now one of the few areas in southern England where the whole range of characteristic species can be seen.

An old windmill on the marshes at Rye

The restored Hever Castle proved too small for the Astors' lavish entertaining and the inspired solution was to build the 'Tudor Village'. This picturesque cluster of apparently individual cottages actually consists of 100 luxurious rooms, linked by corridors and a covered bridge over the moat to the castle.

HEVER CASTLE
Kent

HEVER, 7 MILES (11.5 KM) WEST OF TONBRIDGE

*R*omance, intrigue, wealth, power and far-reaching decisions – all have been played out on the stage of Hever Castle. This was the childhood home of Anne Boleyn, for whom Henry VIII abandoned his wife, his faith and the faith of the nation. Anne's fate is well known, and her parents died, broken, within two years. Henry later gave Hever to his divorced wife Anne of Cleves. Over the centuries Hever went into a decline until, in 1903, it was bought by William Waldorf Astor who spent substantial amounts of his $100 million fortune on restoring the castle to its former magnificence.

Today Hever is as much a monument to early 20th-century craftsmanship as it is to the past. Room after room of splendid panelling and intricate carving blend perfectly with the original timbers. The rooms are furnished with antiques; walls are hung with splendid tapestries, one depicting Princess Mary's marriage to Louis XII of France, with Anne Boleyn reputedly among the attendants; portraits include a Holbein of Henry VIII, and Queen Elizabeth I by John Bettes the Younger. The dark and oppressive Henry VIII Room, with its great four-poster bed, is evocative of the period, but the most poignant is Anne Boleyn's Room, containing the prayer book she took with her to her execution.

Open from mid-March to October every afternoon. Tel: 01732 865224.

A romantic castle, once the home of Anne Boleyn

PENSHURST PLACE
Kent

PENSHURST, 4½ MILES (7 KM) NORTH-WEST OF TUNBRIDGE WELLS

Penshurst Place represents an intriguing blend of architectural styles

The original part of Penshurst Place was built between 1340 and 1345 for Sir John de Pulteney, and although it was extended and modified by successive owners its magnificent baron's hall is superbly preserved. This was the heart of the medieval house, where the entire household lived beneath the wonderful chestnut-beamed roof; its central fireplace is still evident today. It is the oldest and the finest example of a medieval hall in the country.

Penshurst was closely connected with royalty, belonging at one time to Henry IV's third son, and later to Henry VIII. His son, Edward VI, gave the property to Sir William Sidney in 1552 and it is still the Sidney family home.

A great variety of architectural styles are incorporated in the building we see today, though its battlemented exterior presents a unified face, and its series of interesting rooms provides a splendid backdrop for the superb furniture, crystal chandeliers, tapestries and works of art. There are family portraits everywhere, including one of that famous ancestor, Sir Philip Sidney, the great Elizabethan soldier, courtier and poet. A tremendous amount of restoration work has been carried out since World War II, when Penshurst was damaged by flying bombs, and it is as much a monument to the most recent generations of Sidneys as to its great figures of the past.

Open from Easter to October every afternoon. Tel: 01892 870307.

GREAT COMP
Kent

BOROUGH GREEN, 7 MILES (11 KM) EAST OF SEVENOAKS

Sited in the beautiful wooded countryside of the Weald of Kent, Great Comp gardens surround a 17th-century house. Mr and Mrs Roderick Cameron originally bought an area of 4$^1/_2$ acres (2ha), but land was added in 1962 and 1975 so that today the gardens cover 7$^1/_2$ acres (3ha). Considerable devastation was caused by the great storms of 1987 and 1990, but Great Comp remains a successful combination of a plantsman's garden, with over 3000 named plants (including no fewer than 30 varieties of magnolia), and one of changing vistas employing curving walks through colourful woodland and focal points such as a group of ruins, a temple and several urns.

Entering on the north side of the garden you come on to a spacious lawn sloping up to a top terrace. Viburnums predominate in the shrub and herbaceous border, and the old yew, *Taxus baccata*, is thought to be more than 150 years old. Two young ginkgoes stand on either side of the steps with a *Photinia x fraseri* close by. The borders here are planted in a cottage-garden style, and although you would expect to find plants like phloxes and violas in such a setting,

The back of the house overlooks an expanse of well kept lawn, deeply cut with beds and borders

angel's fishing rods, crocosmias and yuccas are, perhaps, more of a surprise. Several berberis make an attractive impact, as does golden sage, variegated thyme and rue. On the top path the planting of the borders is rich, with colourful azaleas, hydrangeas, Japanese witch hazel and many varieties of magnolia. In the woodland in this eastern part of the garden are a tall silver birch, *Pinus sylvestris* 'Aurea' and a red oak, while beyond a fine American dogwood is a splendid young dawn redwood.

One of the pleasures of Great Comp is the sudden appearance of long views in the depths of beautiful woodland. From the Lion Summerhouse, a tastefully converted privy, there is a splendid view of the garden's 'Place de l'Etoile', embellished with a Doulton urn. In the same area, the 'ruins' were created 15 years ago, and conifers, heathers and rock plants enhance their picturesque effect. At the garden's southern boundary a long, straight path joins the Vine urn with the Temple, and from this vantage point you can see both winter and summer heathers. The shrub planting includes the American smoke bush, and *Pinus coulteri* with its abnormally long needles. Near the Temple, erected in 1973, is a wonderful weeping pear, as well as a Nootka cypress.

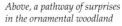

Returning to the house a *Magnolia x veitchii* can be seen underplanted with hostas, ferns, irises, lysimachia and polygonum, and in the herbaceous borders in the Square, plume poppies, pink, yellow and white achillea, sedums, euonymus, yuccas and begonias add their seasonal colour.

Open daily, from April to October. Tel: 01732 882669.

Above, a pathway of surprises in the ornamental woodland

Below, a hydrangea has been underplanted and invaded by brilliant nasturtiums

Deal Castle, where Iron Age weapons and relics of Deal's history are displayed

---

DEAL CASTLE
Kent

DEAL, 9 MILES (14.5 KM) NORTH-EAST OF DOVER

The Cinque Ports
Walmer is the official residence of the Lords Warden of the Cinque Ports, a commercial alliance of south coast ports dating from the 11th century. Winston Churchill held this office between 1941 and 1965, and the present holder is HM Queen Elizabeth The Queen Mother.

*I*n 1533 Henry VIII, disappointed at not having produced a healthy son, divorced his Catholic wife, Catherine of Aragon. This move resulted not only in Henry being excommunicated, but also brought him in direct conflict with Catholic France and Spain. In order to protect England's southern coasts, Henry built a series of forts, financed largely from the proceeds of the dissolved monasteries.

Deal and nearby Walmer are two of these forts, both plain, functional buildings, where the sole purpose was defence. At Deal, six semi-circular bastions are joined to form a tower, which is further protected by an outer wall of the same shape. All were liberally supplied with gun loops and cannon ports, so that, in all, an attacker faced five tiers of guns. Walmer has a simpler plan, involving a circular tower and a quatrefoil outer wall, but the defensive principle is the same, and from every angle an invader would face a bristling armoury of handguns and cannon.

As it happened, Henry's precautions were not necessary and Deal was not attacked until 1648, when it was held for Charles I in the Civil War. It suffered extensive damage, but was not attacked again until a bomb fell on it during World War II.

Open all year, but closed on Monday and Tuesday between November and March. Tel: 01304 372762.

LEEDS CASTLE
Kent

5 MILES (8 KM) EAST OF MAIDSTONE

*L*eeds Castle is not, as many would-be visitors might suppose, in the city of Leeds in West Yorkshire, but in the depths of the beautiful Kent countryside. It takes its name from its first owner, a man named Leed, or Ledian, who built himself a wooden castle in 857. Leed was the Chief Minister of the King of Kent, and in a time where a fall from grace or an attack by rival parties was a way of life, Leed was very wise in building a stronghold for his family on the two small islands in the lake formed by the River Len.

It is difficult to imagine what the original Leeds Castle must have looked like, especially when confronted by the grandeur of the building that stands on the two islands today. Edward I rebuilt the earlier Norman castle, providing it with a set of outer walls, a barbican, and the curious 'gloriette', a D-shaped tower on the smaller of the two islands, which was altered extensively in the Tudor period. Much of Leeds Castle was restored and rebuilt in the 19th century, and many of the rooms are open to the public, all lavishly decorated, with superb collections of art and furniture.

Open daily April to October, weekends only in winter. Tel: 01622 765400.

Leeds Castle has, in one of its out-buildings, a most unusual museum dedicated to medieval dog collars.

Leeds Castle, set in 500 acres of landscaped parkland, has been beautifully restored

The west tower of the church, a survival from the 13th century

APPLEDORE
Kent

10 MILES (16 KM) SOUTH OF ASHFORD

This peaceful and attractive village on the edge of Romney Marsh started life as a port on the estuary of the River Rother, but in the 13th century violent storms changed the course of the Rother and gradual silting-up left Appledore (meaning 'apple tree') 8 miles (13km) or so inland. Not far enough, however, to escape a raid by the French in 1380 during which they burned the 13th-century church. Its chunky tower survived and the rest was reconstructed shortly afterwards, a little untidily, making plentiful use of timber inside. In 1381 Wat Tyler attacked Horne's Place, a 14th-century farmhouse with a gem of a private chapel. More peaceful days followed, with markets and a fair that had been licensed by Edward III being held in its broad, grassy main street. In 1804 there was the threat of another French invasion, under Napoleon, and the Royal Military Canal was built, curving round the marsh. Regular bends meant the whole stretch could be covered by cannon fire. The canal's potential was not forgotten in World War II, when pillboxes were built along its length. Today, Appledore lies quietly to the north of the canal, most of it along the one main street, its buildings a pleasing mix of styles and ages from the 16th century onwards.

AYLESFORD
Kent

3 MILES (5 KM) NORTH-WEST OF MAIDSTONE

There is a record of a bridge spanning the Medway at Aylesford in 1287. In the 14th century this was replaced by the Kentish flagstone bridge that has survived to this day. The view from this bridge is one of the best there is of the picturesque brick-and-half-timbered, steeply gabled cottages. The river once powered the paper mill that has operated here since the turn of the century. Prehistory courses through the veins of this, one of Kent's oldest villages. On the outskirts is Kit's Coty House, the awe-inspiring remains of a Neolithic burial chamber. In AD455 the Britons were defeated in battle here by Jutish invaders, and in 893 the Danes were seen off by King Alfred, while in 918 Edmund Ironside routed Canute and the Vikings. Later, in more peaceful mode, the Carmelites came to England and founded their first friary in this country in Aylesford, in 1240. For 300 years it flourished, until it was given, at the dissolution, to Ann Boleyn's lover, Sir Thomas Wyatt of nearby Allington. The estate stayed in private hands until 1949 when the dispossessed order of Carmelites returned to their home (the first to do so), finding many of the buildings still standing although in need of repair. Fully restored, The Friars' 14th-century cloister, 15th-century Pilgrims' Hall and pottery are open to the public.

The flower of Carmel once cut down now flourishes more luxuriantly than ever. (Inscription over the entrance to the main courtyard of The Friars)

On the banks of the Medway, a little-known but attractive waterway

DOVER CASTLE
Kent

DOVER, 7 MILES (11.5 KM) EAST OF FOLKESTONE

Within the castle grounds are a Roman lighthouse and a beautiful little Anglo-Saxon church.

Below, rich in history, Dover Castle was used during World War II to plan the evacuation of Dunkirk

Below right, the Saxon church of St Mary de Castros

*D*over Castle is so enormous, and contains so many fascinating features, that it is difficult to know where to start in its description. It was a state-of-the-art castle in medieval times, displaying some of the most highly advanced defensive architecture available. Its strategically vital position at the point where England is nearest to the coast of France has given it a unique place in British history. And it is simultaneously powerful, massive, imposing and splendid.

The castle stands on a spur of rock overlooking the English Channel. The entire site is protected by walls bristling with towers and bulwarks. These include the formidable Constable's Gate, erected in the 1220s, a pair of D-shaped towers that not only served as a serious obstacle for would-be invaders, but provided comfortable lodgings for the castle constables (or, nowadays, their deputies). Outside the walls are earthworks and natural slopes that provide additional defence.

The castle was begun by William the Conqueror, but the great keep was built by Henry II in the 1180s. It is surrounded by yet another wall, studded with square towers and two barbicans. The keep itself is 95 feet (29m) tall, and around 95 feet (29m) across at its base. There are square turrets at each corner, and even at the top of the tower, where the walls are thinnest, they are still 17 feet (5.2m) thick. The well is carved into the thickness of the wall, and plunges 240 feet (73m) to reach a steady water supply.

Dover has had a rich and eventful history, and one especially important episode occurred during the last year of the reign of King John (1216). John's barons had been growing increasingly frustrated with him, and had invited Prince Louis, heir to the French throne, to invade England and take over. Louis landed at Dover and laid siege to Dover Castle, which was held by Hubert de Burgh, a baron loyal to John. Ever since the castle was founded, kings had laid down vast sums of money for its repair and development (notably Henry II and Richard I), and it looked as though this investment had paid off. Louis, it seemed, would be unable to breach Dover's powerful walls. Then the unthinkable happened – the French managed to take the outer barbican and undermine the gate. Despite de Burgh's efforts, Louis was poised to enter the inner enclosure. With fortunate timing, John died, the barons proclaimed allegiance to his successor, Henry III, and Louis went home. Lessons were learned, however, and Henry spent a good deal of money in improving Dover's defences.

Open all year daily, except Christmas and New Year. Tel: 01304 823292.

Rochester Castle's well was 65 feet (20m) deep, and was constructed so that water could be drawn up from any of the keep's four floors.

ROCHESTER CASTLE
Kent

ROCHESTER, 10 MILES (16 KM) NORTH OF MAIDSTONE

The magnificent Norman keep at Rochester has seen more than its share of battles and sieges, but perhaps the most famous one was in 1215. Shortly after the barons forced King John to sign the Magna Carta, he turned against them in a bitter war. Rochester Castle was held for the barons, and John laid siege to it with incredible ferocity. The siege lasted for about seven weeks, during which time those in the castle were reduced to a diet of horsemeat and water. Meanwhile, John kept a constant barrage of missiles from crossbows and ballistas (stone-throwing machines), and began to dig a tunnel under the keep

The massive Norman keep of Rochester Castle

itself. Part of the keep collapsed, but the defenders bravely fought on. Those men who could no longer fight were sent out, whereupon it is said John had their hands and feet cut off. But Rochester finally fell, and the defenders were imprisoned.

Building on the keep started in about 1127, and it is one of the largest in England. Its walls soar to 113 feet (34m) and are up to 12 feet (3.7m) thick. Although this was first and foremost a defensive building, there are some beautifully carved archways and windows.

Open all year daily, except Christmas and New Year. Tel: 01634 402276.

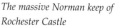

CHILHAM
Kent

5 MILES (8 KM) SOUTH-WEST OF CANTERBURY

Narrow lanes climb up through Kentish hills and orchards to open out unexpectedly into Chilham's village square, one of Kent's show-pieces and often used as a film set. Chilham is used to visitors; for 350 years, after Thomas à Becket's murder, travellers used to pass through on The Pilgrims' Way from Winchester and London to his shrine in Canterbury Cathedral. Nowadays it is on the North Downs Way. Best appreciated out of season, its square is a delightfully haphazard mix of gabled, half-timbered houses, shops and inns dating from the late Middle Ages. Some were refaced in brick in the 18th century. Streets lead down from the corners, each lined with more old houses, some of them overhanging. At either end of the square are the church and the castle. St Mary's stands behind the 15th-century White Horse Inn, built of flint and stone and dominated by its Perpendicular west tower. The castle consists of a Norman keep built on Roman foundations and a Jacobean mansion built by Sir Dudley Digges, a high-ranking official of James I. The lodge gates in the square were added earlier this century, and the grounds laid out by Charles I's gardener, John Tradescant, but reworked by 'Capability' Brown in the 18th century. They are open to the public and now house a sanctuary for birds of prey.

In the church is a large monument by the prolific sculptor Francis Chantrey (1781–1841). It was his fortune that founded the art collection that is now housed in London's Tate Gallery.

Tudor houses include one with a bell-tower, named Pilgrims' Cottage

In the sheds at New Romney station, the railway's headquarters

ROMNEY, HYTHE & DYMCHURCH RAILWAY
Kent

HYTHE, 4½ MILES (7.5 KM) SOUTH OF FOLKESTONE

Miniature railways have a fascination of their own, not least for children, witnessed by the enduring popularity of the Romney, Hythe & Dymchurch Railway since it opened in 1927. Although the number of miniature railways has mushroomed since World War II, the concept of the Romney, Hythe and Dymchurch remains unique. The reason for this is largely to due to its creator, Captain Jack Howey, who had the wealth to build a main line railway in miniature, with double track, substantial stations and powerful locomotives capable of a scale speed of 75mph (120kph).

A strong commercial case for such lavishness would be hard to make – no miniature railway of comparable length has been able to justify more than a single line, for example. But with the rental income from a good chunk of central Melbourne in

Australia, Captain Howey did not have to worry about sceptical bank managers. To power his trains, Howey ordered nine steam locomotives, five based on the elegant Pacific design by Sir Nigel Gresley for the London & North Eastern Railway, two freight types for aggregate traffic that never materialised and a pair of Canadian-style Pacifics – Howey particularly enjoyed his railway holidays there.

The Duke of York, later King George VI, drove the first train into New Romney and the railway soon became well known as the World's Smallest Public Railway. It flourished during the 1930s and played its part in the defence of the Kent coast when an armoured train was built, sporting a couple of machine guns and an anti-tank rifle. Powered by a protected 4-8-2, *Samson*, it made regular forays from its dummy hill near Dymchurch.

Some economies were made on the railway as the popularity of holidays abroad eroded its traffic during the 1960s, but new management following Howey's death has helped to revive the railway's fortunes, and it remains one of the finest miniature railways in the world. Amongst many innovations is an observation car equipped with licensed bar. As well as being a tourist attraction, the Romney, Hythe & Dymchurch has a practical role in the community: since 1977 it has carried about 200 children a day from the Dymchurch area to and from school in New Romney.

Hythe is the largest resort on the line, with some fine Victorian hotels, and the terminal station still has the only original overall roof spanning its three platforms. It stands beside the Royal Military Canal, built to deter invasion by Napoleon. The station's size, coupled with the water tower, signal box, turntable and engine shed

The locomotive No 8, Hurricane (below) was temporarily renamed in 1994 after accidental damage

(now disused) help to create a main line atmosphere. As the long train gathers pace under the signal gantry at the platform end, the line is fringed by back gardens on one side and the remains of the canal on the other. The pace quickens as the line enters open country with wide views over the flat land of Romney Marsh, renowned for smuggling activities following the decline of the Cinque ports. In the distance can be seen the gently rising hills of Lympne, with its extraordinary castle built for Sir Philip Sassoon.

Bowling along the flat land towards Dymchurch at about 25mph (40kph), the clickety-clack of the rail joints provides a sound almost consigned to history on all but secondary routes on British Rail. After one of the line's many level crossings, the train reaches Dungeness, which once had an overall roof, signal box and sidings. On the approach to the next station at

Jefferstone Lane, look out for the bungalow in which E Nesbit spent the last years of her life, having achieved fame with *The Railway Children*; it is on the left as you enter the station and is named 'The Long Boat'.

Open fields, a shallow cutting and a tunnel under a main road precede the railway's headquarters at New Romney. Apart from the attraction of watching engines coming off shed or shunting carriages, the station has a popular model exhibition with showcase models and two impressive model railways. Although the station has a huge new roof spanning the running lines, elements of Howey's original station survive, including the wooden clock tower.

Wartime damage to the line between New Romney and Dungeness wrecked the track so badly that the second line was never replaced. Now trains can cross at one point, Romney Sands, on

Hythe station. The town is the largest resort on the line

this section of the line that traverses one of the most unusual areas of Britain. For part of the way the line is fringed by single-storey bungalows at Greatstone, most of them built during the 1930s and many still retaining the architectural character of that decade.

The broad expanse of shingle that surrounds the two nuclear power stations and two lighthouses at Dungeness is for some an alienating and barren landscape. But for anyone with an interest in natural history, it offers a diverse selection of rare plants with colonies of moths and butterflies, and is a sanctuary for birds. Having reached the end of the line, the 1904 lighthouse is a good reason to delay the return to New Romney, with a rewarding panorama from the top.

Train service: daily from April to September and October half-term; weekends in March and first half of October. Tel: 01797 363256.

New Romney, where there are model railways and a model exhibition

Something fresh and local: a fishmonger's in Old High Street

An Island No Longer

Linking Britain to the Continent physically for the first time since the English Channel was formed some 9500 years ago, the Channel Tunnel – actually three tunnels – is one of the 20th century's most exciting engineering achievements. The idea was far from new, and had been suggested in France well over a hundred years ago. A French engineer presented Napoleon Bonaparte with a plan for a tunnel to accommodate horse-drawn carriages, but the English had reason to distrust Napoleon's motives. Work on a tunnel eventually began from both ends in 1877, but was halted after an outcry in England. Digging the present tunnel began in 1986, and the French and English tunnelling parties met and joined hands beneath the Channel on 1 December 1990. On that day Britain ceased to be an island.

FOLKESTONE
Kent

14 MILES (23 KM) EAST OF ASHFORD

The arrival of the South Eastern Railway in 1842 transformed Folkestone from a minor fishing village into a cross-Channel ferry port and one of the south coast's classier resorts. Within a year the first passenger ship had left for Boulogne, taking four hours over the journey, which meant that London-to-Paris could be done in a trifling 12 hours. William Cubitt's 19-arch brick railway viaduct, which takes passengers out to the ferries, has been hailed as the most distinguished piece of architecture in the town. Today, fairground amusements and small boats cluster close to the stone pier. A water-powered cliff lift carries visitors effortlessly up from the foreshore to

the West Cliff and the lawns, flower beds and bandstands of The Leas, a spacious promenade with a Mediterranean air that is almost a mile long ('leas' is a Kentish dialect word for an open space). Handsome terraces and stately hotels gaze out loftily over the Channel in an area originally planned by Decimus Burton. The oldest part of Folkestone clambers steeply uphill immediately inland from the harbour, and the oldest street is probably the Old High Street. The medieval parish church of St Mary and St Eanswythe still contains the bones of Eanswythe, a Kentish princess who founded a nunnery here in the 7th century. The west window is a memorial to Folkestone's most famous

Cobbled and narrow, Old High Street is probably Folkestone's oldest thoroughfare

son, William Harvey, physician to both James I and Charles I, and the discoverer of the circulation of the blood, who was born in Folkestone in 1578. The nearby British Lion pub claims to be one of the oldest in England. Over to the east is the main bathing beach, East Cliff Sands, with a long stretch of open grassland above it, and three Martello towers. Folkestone Warren, now a nature reserve, is a tangled wilderness of tumbled chalk created by a landslip in 1915. Walks zigzag through what is locally known as 'Little Switzerland'. In Cheriton, on Folkestone's northern outskirts, the Eurotunnel Exhibition Centre tells you vividly – and in both English and French – everything there is to be told about the new Channel Tunnel and travelling through it in Le Shuttle. An observation tower commands a panoramic view of the site, and there is one of the largest model railway layouts in the country on display, as well as an array of technology, interactive exhibits and tunnel boring machinery of prodigious proportions.

Flotsam and Jetsam

`At low tide one may walk round by the shore, under the base of the cliffs; but this is laborious going, and the time has to be chosen nicely, or there is a risk of being cut off by the incoming sea. But this adventure has a sort of Robinson Crusoe quality, with its solitude, its discoveries of small items of flotsam and jetsam and unexpected sea-pieces, while the formidable ramparts of chalk rear up, their muscles straining against the constant onslaughts of the tides and storms.'

Richard Church, *Kent* (1948)

Tall white cliffs at St Margaret's Bay guard the narrow sea-passage between England and France

ST MARGARET'S BAY
Kent

4 MILES (6 KM) NORTH-EAST OF DOVER

Steep and narrow, the road twists down to the bay between its white, scrub-tangled cliffs. The terrace of the Coastguard pub is a good spot for watching the shipping in the Channel, and a nearby World War II pillbox still turns a cold stare out to sea. Because this is the nearest point to the French coast, a mere 21 miles (34km) away, it has long been a favourite spot with cross-Channel swimmers. Among the villas on the cliff are the lawns and flowerbeds of The Pines Garden, created here in 1970 to prevent the land being taken for a carpark. A statue of Sir Winston Churchill in bulldog mood by Oscar Nemon keeps watch. A most unusual feature is the grand façade of a 17th-century building from the City of London, which is lying on its back in the grass with flowers growing in the window spaces. Up at the top, the village of St Margaret's at Cliffe gathers round its sturdy Norman church, which is dedicated to St Margaret of Antioch. The local smugglers used to store their tackle in the tower. The South Foreland lighthouse is open to the public on summer weekends, and a granite obelisk on the cliffs to the north honours the Dover Patrol which guarded the Channel throughout the two World Wars.

MARGATE
Kent

15 MILES (24 KM) NORTH-EAST OF CANTERBURY

An engagingly dotty clock tower keeps a benevolent eye on Margate seafront

Margate's reputation as a breezy, boisterous, cheap and cheerful pleasure resort goes back well over 200 years. It was a Margate man, a Quaker glover named Benjamin Beale, who gave the world the bathing machine, which he invented in the 1750s. By 1775 the town marshalled 30 of them drawn up on its fine, curving beach of golden sand. London trippers used to arrive in seasick droves in sailing boats called Margate hoys, of 80 tons or so. In the 19th century these vessels were replaced by steamers, and the railway reached Margate in the l840s. Today the seafront along Marine Terrace is alive with amusement arcades, bingo parlours, palmists, joke shops and souvenir shops, and places to buy fish and chips, ice cream, candy floss and Margate rock. The colossal amusement park has 25 acres (10ha) of rides with all the fun of the fair. The quieter and older part of the town is close to the harbour, the stone pier and the restored classical Droit House (the 'droits' were the harbour dues). There are pleasant old streets here and the local history museum is in the former town hall. Margate caves are a popular attraction, and the underground shell grotto on Grotto Hill is a remarkable 18th-century folly whose walls are encrusted with thousands of sea-shells.

INDEX